Creating an Effective Learning Environment

Learning Styles	Communicating with your Students
Learning Environments	Memory
Motivation and Mistakes	Goal Setting and Success
Mind-mapping and Speed Reading	Nutrition and Learning
Emotions and Learning	The Brain
Developing Intelligence	Teacher Success Tips

With a preface by Julie Anne Stevens

Karen Boyes

To Hamish
May learning be one of the most enjoyable experiences of your life.

Cover and book designer: Susana Siew-Demunck

Published in Australia by

HAWKER BROWNLOW
•
E D U C A T I O N

P.O. Box 580, Moorabbin,
Victoria 3189, Australia
Phone: (03) 9555 1344 Fax: (03) 9553 4538
Toll Free Ph: 1800 33 4603 Fax: 1800 15 0445
Website: http://www.hbe.com.au
Email: orders@hbe.com.au

© 2004 Hawker Brownlow Education

Republished for Outside The Box Learning Resources
Jigginstown Commercial Centre
Newbridge Road, Naas, Co. Kildare, EIRE
Tel: 045 856344 Fax: 045 897819 Mobile: 086 2570604
Email: outsidetheboxlearning@eircom.net or holmesc@eircom.net
URL: www.outsidetheboxlearning.com

Printed in Australia
All rights reserved

ISBN: 1 74101 352 6
Code: EIR3526
0604

Creating an Effective Learning Environment is a resource which gives teachers practical advice on how to make changes to the learning environment so that desired learning outcomes are achieved. The author synthesizes new knowledge about brain theory and its direct impact in the classroom. The Irish Primary School Curriculum of 1999 heralded many changes in the practices of teaching and learning in schools. These changes incorporate current educational thinking and are based on the most innovative and effective pedagogical practices. One of the major underlying principles is that the child is at the centre of the entire process. Another major change to the curriculum is that 'it accords equal importance to what the child learns and to the process by which he or she learns it' (Primary School Curriculum, Introduction, p. 10). Both the Content of Learning and the Process of Learning are equally important. However, content and process changes do not occur in isolation. The link to the learning environment is crucial. The relationship between curriculum differentiation (i.e. content and process changes) and the learning environment are two sides of the one coin. If you make changes to the content or process of learning, changes to the learning environment will occur automatically. It is also possible to approach it from the other perspective. Make changes to the learning environment and changes to the content, processes and outcomes of the curriculum will be facilitated. This book provides valuable tips and ideas on how to influence the learning environment. Along with an understanding of the cognitive and social emotional development of the child, there is also greater recognition in the Primary School Curriculum that children are individuals and a 'one hat fits all' approach may no longer be appropriate. One of the essential features of modern educational thought is 'a recognition of the principle that there are different kinds of learning and that individual children learn in different ways' (Primary School Curriculum Introduction, p. 10). *Creating an Effective Learning Environment* provides a practical guide on different learning styles and how changes can be made in order to accommodate these differences. This book is a valuable and practical resource for all teachers. It supports the Irish Primary Curriculum by developing understanding and awareness of the importance of the Learning Environment.

Julie Anne Stevens B.Ed., C.O.G.E., M. Ed. (Gifted Ed.)

Teacher, Lucan Educate Together Primary School, Dublin

Karen Boyes is the founder, head facilitator and CEO of Spectrum Education Limited, an educational consulting company which specialises in accelerating learning and whole brain learning techniques. She is a highly skilled, enthusiastic and dynamic presenter who has 17 years experience in the field of education. She was also the *Her Business* New Zealand Business Woman of the Year 2001. She has spent the last ten years researching, developing and designing effective training and courses using accelerating learning, whole brain learning techniques and peak performance. Her course experience includes having worked with teachers, parents, students and corporate clients.

Karen is actively involved in the national and international accelerating learning network, and was invited to speak at the 1999 International Accelerating Learning Conference in Texas. Karen is committed to presenting her information in an energetic, exciting manner and will not only educate but inspire and motivate, altering the perception of both learners and learning.

Karen creates an environment where it is fun to learn and safe to make mistakes. This encourages participants to be relaxed and totally involved and is proven to produce outstanding results. Karen uses a unique blend of music, colour, games, stories and activities, giving the students a mixture of learning tools and improved self-awareness. Using this new information maximises the yearn to learn and the ability to recall and retain information. Thousands of students throughout Australasia have benefited from these techniques and have gone on to score well beyond what they thought they were capable of at exam time.

Thousands of teachers have also benefited from Karen's teacher workshops. Participants come away from these workshops re-energised and motivated to go back into the classroom and integrate the information with a renewed passion and vigour.

When Karen's focus of 'how' rather than just 'what' to teach and learn is manifested in the classroom by both teacher and student, the whole education process becomes clearer, more successful, less stressful, more fun and far more rewarding for all involved.

At the corporate level, Karen works in the areas of motivation, effective communication, and attaining and maintaining peak performance. Together these create a friendly, fun environment where superior results are achieved by working smarter rather than harder, with less stress and increased teamwork.

Acknowledgements

This book could not have been possible without the many people who have knowingly and unknowingly assisted me on my journey of life.

I'd like to thank Sandy Roydhouse, my editor, for her skill and patience in putting this book together. Without her guidance, it would still be a dream. Thanks also to Belinda Clune for all her fabulous illustrations.

Secondly I'd like to thank the team at Spectrum Education, both past and present: Trudy Blair, Suzanne Hodder, Janet Nixon, Rachel Tobin; Gavin Fieldes, Marion Miller and Lara Phegan. Thanks for believing in my dream, to make education fun and fulfilling for all.

Thanks also to my business coach, Kevin Heppleston from Action International, for keeping me on track and encouraging me to continually expand my boundaries.

A special thanks to my biggest supporters, you, my clients; successful teachers, whose success and enthusiasm has built my success, and whose questions have helped me learn and grow.

Thanks to my many teachers: Pearl Sidwell, Glenn Capelli, Gordon Dryden, Tony Robbins, Michael Gerber, Robert Kiyosaki, Bobbie DePorter, Blair Singer, Wayne Morgan, Brent Stubbins, Kirsty Hayes, Eric Jensen, Brad Sugars, Carla Hannaford, Michael Wall, Michael Boyd, and all of those teachers whose books, tapes and seminars have inspired and motivated me to keep going. A big thanks also to my dear friend Bronwyn, for your hours of support and love.

Most of all I'd like to thank my parents, Tui and Trevor, who have always supported me with amazing commitment and believed in me in ways that can never be put in words. And to my sister, Cheryl, for her ability to get what she wants from life. Thanks.

Finally to Denny whose love and support is beyond compare. You have taught me so much – particularly how to have balance in my life. Thanks for being the best dad to our son Hamish and for being the best husband in the world. I love you.

Acknowledgements

Contents

Introduction . . . . **xii**

Chapter 1:
Learning Styles **1**
- Learning Styles 2
- Visual Learners 2
- Auditory Learners 5
- Kinesthetic Learners 9
- Olfactory Learners 13
- Gustatory Learners 14
- Catering for Styles in your Classroom 15

Chapter 2:
Communicating with your Students . . **17**
- VAK Communication 18
- Matcher and Mismatcher 20
- Impulsive and Reflective Learners 22
- Global and Analytical Learners 25
- Sequential and Random Learners 26
- Internally- and Externally-Referenced Learners 28
- Concrete and Abstract Learners 29

Chapter 3:
Learning Environments **31**
- Colour 32
- Lights 33
- Temperature 34
- Plants 34
- Music or Silence 34
- Food and Water 38
- Structure 38
- Social Environment 39

© 2004 Hawker Brownlow Education EIR3526

Chapter 4:
Memory 41

- The Brain 42
- The Seven Keys to Memory 43
- Internal Processing 46
- Memory in the Classroom 8
- Memory and Spelling 50

Chapter 5:
Motivation and Mistakes 53

- Affirmations 55
- Physiology 57
- Making Mistakes 59
- Four Levels of Learning 60
- Motivation and Rewards 61

Chapter 6:
Goal Setting and Success 67

- Goal Setting 68
- The Cycle of Success 70
- Attitude 72
- Visualisation 73
- The Pygmalion Effect 74
- Words to Avoid when Aiming for Success 74

Chapter 7:
Mind Mapping and Speed Reading . . 77

- Mind Mapping 78
- Speed Reading 80

Contents

Chapter 8:

Nutrition and Learning 83

- The Importance of Protein 84
- Vitamins and Minerals 84
- Iron 85
- Fat 85
- Water 85
- Snacking vs Three Meals per Day 86
- What Can I Do in my Classroom? 86

Chapter 9:

Emotions and Learning 89

- The Role of Emotions in Learning 90
- Value Every Effort 93
- Laughter Boosts Learning 93

Chapter 10:

Understanding the Brain 95

- Left and Right Brain 96
- The Triune Brain 96
- Mental Fitness 97
- Ages and Stages of Brain Development 99
- Reading and Writing: What's Appropriate 101

Chapter 11:

Developing Intelligence 103

- Lateral Thinking 104
- What is Intelligent Behaviour? 106
- Multiple Intelligences 113

Chapter 12:
Teacher Success Tips. 123

- Time Management 124
- Dealing with Stress Effectively 127
- Sleep. 129

Reference List 132

Suggested Reading 134

Contents

Introduction

The twenty-first century is changing so fast. Sixty-five percent of the thirteen-year-olds in our schools today will be going into jobs that haven't been invented yet. It is predicted that students will have up to five different careers in their lifetime. It currently takes four years to train to be an engineer. After working for two years, 60 per cent of what was learned at university will be obsolete (Jukes 2003).

What we, as teachers and educators, can no longer do is give students skills for particular jobs and employment. Who knows what the world will look like in the year 2040? However, what we can give our students is the learning-to-learn strategies. If they know how to learn, quickly and efficiently, learn from their mistakes and have high self-esteem, they will have the competitive advantage over someone who can't. Teaching how to learn and self-esteem has to be our priority.

As you read and pick up ideas through this book, please be aware of some fabulous life advice, from the cabin crew of an aeroplane. Before take-off the cabin crew gives a safety demonstration. They say, 'If a mask appears like this before you, adjust your own mask first, before adjusting anybody else's.' This is great advice. Before you rush off to use these ideas and strategies in your classroom, please pause and consider how you can use them for yourself, to adopt new ways of working and to make your teaching easier and more efficient.

In his book, *Seven Habits of Highly Effective Families*, Stephen Covey gives advice to parents. He says, 'You are not bringing up your children, you are bringing up your grandchildren.' I believe that this is true of teaching today. We're not teaching the children in the classroom, we're teaching the next generation. Teaching used to be the most revered profession in the universe, and I still think it is. The average person, in their lifetime, affects the lives of over one hundred thousand people. A teacher will affect the lives of over one million people. You don't just affect the students in your classroom, you affect their home and in turn their workplace. Teaching is such an exciting profession, working and shaping the next generation.

Your effect, as a teacher, is not just for the year the students are in your class. It can be for many, many years afterwards. There are still teachers from your past, affecting you today. Your effect is lifelong.

A final thought is a quote from Confucius.

> *'If you want to plan for one year, plant rice,*
> *if you want to plan for ten years, plant trees*
> *and if you want to plan for one hundred years,*
> *educate children.'*

Chapter 1

Learning Styles

- Learning Styles

- Visual Learners

- Auditory Learners

- Kinesthetic Learners

- Olfactory Learners

- Gustatory Learners

- Catering for Styles in your Classroom

Chapter 1

Understanding and valuing different learning styles within the classroom is paramount for successful teaching in your classroom.

Learning Styles

According to the Bandler and Grinder model (1991), there are five learning styles – visual, auditory, kinesthetic, olfactory and gustatory – although the first three are more evident in the classroom. It is important to note that everyone displays all of these characteristics some of the time, and that our individual learning style can change according to many different factors. Most people, however, have a dominant mode of learning or one that they prefer. While there are many different tests devised to determine a person's dominant learning style, I prefer to determine styles, including my own, by observation rather than using testing methods.

As well as in the context of teaching and learning, our learning styles are evident in our everyday life – from the way we eat, to the way we buy clothes, and even the way we wash the dishes. Observe your own behaviour and that of those around you … and let the fun begin!

V   isual

A   uditory

K   inesthetic

O   lfactory

G   ustatory

Visual Learners

Visual learners learn by watching and noticing. They typically sit up straight and watch your every move. As a teacher moves from one side of the room to the other the visual learner just follows with their eyes. It is this learner type that spends an extra moment checking their appearance in the mirror before they leave home. These learners are frequently considered the 'good' learners, as they seem to pay attention more often. Visual learners generally have a higher success rate than other learner types because they are able to process information at a faster rate.

Visual Characteristics

- sit up straight

- follow the teacher with their eyes

- speak quickly

- good long-range planners and organisers

- appearance-oriented in both dress and presentation

- good spellers – they can actually see the words in their minds

- memorise by visual association

- not usually distracted by noise

- neat and orderly

- would rather demonstrate than speak

- like art more than music

- often know what to say but can't think of the right words

- sometimes 'tune out' when they mean to pay attention

- forget to relay verbal messages to others

- have trouble remembering verbal instructions, such as directions, unless they are written down

- strong, fast readers

Teaching Ideas

Use a variety of colours in your presentations. As a general rule, charts and posters should have a minimum of two colours.

Write the key points from your lessons on an A1 size piece of paper and hang this in the classroom for learners to refer to.

When giving instructions, write them on the board for learners to refer back to.

When talking about two ways of doing a task or two ideas, hold up two fingers so the visuals can see as well as hear what you're saying.

When giving instructions demonstrate what you would like your learners to do so they can see what it is you are asking. For example, when asking a learner to turn to page 15, show them what page 15 looks like.

Use diagrams and pictures to explain concepts and new ideas. Add colour to show areas that link.

Set up displays with books, posters, activities and any relevant information, for any curriculum area.

Revive the old film projector and your learners can enjoy watching and reading old film strips. They can write captions for films without text and create their own film strip.

Teaching Ideas

Teach your learners how to mindmap. This is a great way for them to record ideas and present work.

ooo

Photocopy books onto acetate and allow your learners to read these from the overhead projector.

✦✦✦

Encourage learners to use different colours and mediums to write with – pens, coloured pencils and markers. Recent research suggests that when learners use their favourite colours, memory and recall are enhanced.

❊❊❊

Allow your learners to express themselves through different art mediums. They may like to paint, draw or sketch their ideas.

Make your posters and charts different shapes and sizes.

)()()(

Vary the volume, pitch, tone and speed of your voice when talking for periods of time. Whisper instructions.

Auditory Learners

Auditory learners learn by listening and discussing. They may appear to be not listening and gazing out the window, but they will usually follow your movements by turning their dominant ear towards you. They often find it distracting to look at the same time as they are listening.

ACTIVITY

Ask someone to talk while they are throwing a ball up and down. Watch and listen carefully. Is it hard to listen while looking? Is the ball distracting? If you said yes, then you have experienced what it is like for an auditory learner when asked to look.

Auditory learners record what they hear on a tape in their head. When they want to recall, they simply rerun the tape. However, if the tape has been programmed in your (the teacher's) voice, they may need to hear your voice again to reactivate it. For example, in a test a learner may ask you to read the question and as soon as you say the first two words, the learner says, 'Stop, I understand.' What they mean is, your voice has activated their tape. If the learner doesn't have your voice to start the tape, say in ten year's time, then the information is unlikely to be retrieved. It is important for the learner to record all information in their own voice by means of discussion.

Often the way information is processed is the only way it can be recalled for an auditory learner. For example, if you teach that, 'The capital of France is Paris' and the learner is tested, '_____ is the capital of France', then the re-ordering of the question does not start the tape and the learner has difficulty answering the question.

Auditory learners may appear to be slower to answer questions but they are often simply rewinding their tape.

ACTIVITY

Chances are that you learned the alphabet by singing the abc song. If so, you have learned it the auditory way. If I asked you, 'What letter comes just after h? s? f? and n? you should be able to answer straight away. If I asked you which letter comes just before m? j? f? and w? you may have to rerun the tape to find out. That is start at abcd ... or mnop ... Have a go ...

Auditory Characteristics

- speak rhythmically
- follow speaker with their ear
- can repeat back and mimic tone, pitch and timbre
- remember what you said word for word six weeks previously
- good at imitating voices
- talk to themselves while working

- easily distracted by noise
- move their lips and pronounce words as they read
- enjoy reading aloud and listening to stories
- find writing difficult and are better at telling
- frequently eloquent speakers
- like music more than art
- learn by listening and remembering what was discussed
- talkative, love discussion and go into lengthy descriptions
- have problems with projects that involve visualisation such as cutting pieces that fit together
- spell better out loud than in written form
- good at remembering and telling jokes

Teaching Ideas

Allow frequent time for discussion, both teacher-directed and with peers. As a rule of thumb, ask learners to discuss and come up with examples each time you teach them a new concept. Allow time for discussion – from 2–10 minutes.

Play quiet music in the background. Baroque is best as it calms the brain and makes learning easier. Be sure to have times with and without music.

Give learners who do not like background noise a pair of headphones to wear. This will create a quiet place for them. Ensure you can get their attention, especially for emergencies.

Give learners opportunities to debate topics. They may like to have debating teams or class councils.

Encourage learners to record information on tape. They may wish to record their ideas, a topic presentation or an interview.

Provide opportunities for learners to listen to material recorded on tape or record information onto a tape and listen to it regularly.

Provide opportunities for learners to make up rhymes, chants and jingles about information they need to learn.

Provide a quiet area in your classroom so learners know they can go to this area and not be distracted.

Bring in guest speakers who will interest your learners. Limit the time your guest speaks so learners don't get restless.

Kinesthetic Learners

There are two types of kinesthetic learner – the tactile/movement-oriented learner and the feeling-oriented learner. Tactile/movement learners are the fidgeters and wrigglers. They have a high need to touch anything and everything. In the junior classroom these learners are the hair plaiters and leg strokers. In a secondary classroom, these are the students who get out of their seats six times during the lesson, drum on their desks, click pens and rock on their chairs. Feeling-oriented kinesthetics are involved with their own feelings. These learners want to be comfortable and feel loved, safe and so on. They enjoy lying on the floor or on a soft cushion while working.

Part of my conditioning as a teacher was that learners needed to be sitting up straight and looking to learn. This is natural for visual learners but kinesthetic learners are at a disadvantage when they have to sit still. A kinesthetic learner finds it very challenging to sit still and actually concentrates on the act of sitting still rather than the lesson content. In the army, soldiers are taught to wiggle their toes when they are required to sit or stand still.

Kinesthetic/Tactile Characteristics

- speak slowly and loudly
- challenged by sitting still
- respond to physical rewards
- touch people to get their attention
- stand close when talking to someone
- physically oriented and move a lot
- learn by manipulating objects and doing
- memorise by walking and seeing
- use a finger as a pointer when reading and gesture a lot
- remember geography when they have actually been there
- may have messy handwriting
- want to act things out
- like being involved in games

Teaching Ideas

Allow learners to move while they are working: read while walking or bouncing on a mini trampoline; dance, clap, jump, pace out while learning new information. (I like to sit on my exercycle to read.)

Provide foam balls or soft toys for learners to hold during discussion and listening times.

■■■

Touch a learner when giving instructions or helping them to understand information. (A safe zone to touch is on the upper arm.) If it is not appropriate to touch a learner, touch their belongings – their book or their pencil case.

☺☺☺

Provide cushions for learners to sit and lie on.

Encourage learners to do role-plays and drama.

♦♦♦

Provide games and activities to reinforce learning.

⊙⊙⊙

Encourage participation in finger rhymes and puppet shows.

●●●

Create activity centres, experiments and projects for learners to complete.

Allow learners to lie on the floor or sit under tables when working.

♦♦♦

Take some old paintbrushes and a bucket of water outside and do printing on the walls.

Kinesthetic/Feeling Characteristics

- dress for comfort
- slouch in their chairs
- prefer to sit or lie on the floor
- quick to notice temperature changes
- may like to read or work under the tables as this gives them a feeling of safety and warmth

 Teaching Ideas

Shift the rubbish bin, shoes and any awful smells away from the door or workspaces.

⊙⊙⊙

Place pot pourri by the door.

■■■

Freshen up your room using an air freshener spray – ensure it doesn't smell like one regularly used in a toilet.

❋❋❋

Place cotton wool soaked in essential oil above the door frame.

♦♦♦

Place a couple of drops of oil on the heater instead of using an oil burner.

〰〰〰

Use basil, rosemary and lemon essential oils to increase concentration and improve memory. Use peppermint oil to stimulate and encourage clear thinking, and lemon to increase productivity.

♌♌♌

Have a vase of fresh flowers in the classroom.

♦♦♦

Purchase a terracotta light bulb ring. Fit this around a standard light bulb and pour a couple of drops of essential oil into it. When the bulb gets warm the smell spreads through the classroom.

Olfactory Learners

Smell is the olfactory sense. Studies show the first thing we notice, subconsciously, when we walk into a room is the temperature. The second thing we notice is the smell. So what do you have by the door of your classroom? The rubbish bin? Children's shoes? What messages are your learners receiving when they walk into your room?

Smell is a fascinating sense. Did you know that a way to sell a house is to have bread baking in the oven and a pot of freshly brewed coffee on the kitchen bench? Top real estate agents say a house that smells of these homely smells will sell nine times out of ten over one that doesn't smell good.

How are sausages sold at a sausage sizzle? By the smell of the onions cooking.

Smell is the only sense not filtered by the brain. It goes directly to the long term memory. What smells trigger memories for you?

When using aromatherapy oils in your classroom, remember to allow the smells in your room to be very subtle so you don't overpower your learners and be aware of those with asthma or other allergies. Useful aromatherapy oils to use in the classroom include rosemary, peppermint, lemon and basil. (Ensure these cannot be touched or swallowed.)

Teaching Ideas

After I had alerted my learners and parents to the foods that are important for learning, and the reasons why, I allowed them to bring food into the classroom to eat at appropriate times. For example, it was not appropriate to eat an apple in the middle of an instructional lesson but it was when the learners were working on their own. Children seemed happier, and more on-task behaviour was displayed.

■ ■ ■

Many learners will learn concepts faster and easier when they are related to food. For example, instead of 7 – 3 =? ask, 'If you had 7 Moro bars and I took 3 away, how many would you have left?'

☺☺☺

Teach students how to write an essay by the hamburger technique: the top bun is the introduction, the filling is the content of your essay and the bottom bun is the conclusion. And obviously, the more filling, the better the hamburger.

Some learners have a high need for chewing and will chew anything they can find, from pens to paper to their hair. Allow these learners to graze throughout the day.

Change your bell times to allow students to eat more often.

Gustatory Learners

The gustatory sense relates to taste. Babies are gustatory learners. When they are given something they immediately put it into their mouth to make sense of it. (This is also because the lips are the most sensitive part of the body.)

Food is becoming more widely accepted as an important part of learning. Studies show children's blood sugar levels cycle every 45 minutes (90 minutes in adults). This means approximately 45 minutes after children have eaten (60 minutes for a teenager) their blood sugar levels will be at a low. This makes thinking harder and slower. Encourage your learners to eat healthy 'brain food' often, throughout the day, to enable them to maintain their learning.

Examples of 'brain foods' include:
- unsalted nuts
- fish, chicken
- fruit and vegetables
- unsalted, plain popcorn.

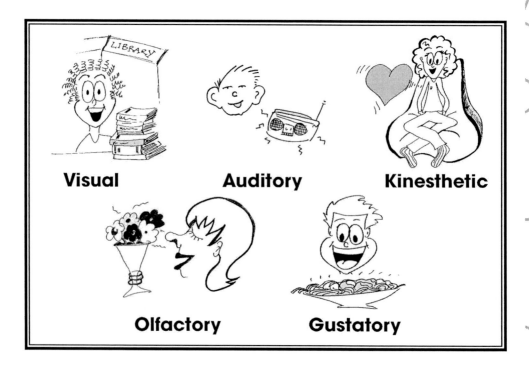

Visual   **Auditory**   **Kinesthetic**

Olfactory   **Gustatory**

Many studies show that protein is more beneficial to the brain than carbohydrates, as carbohydrates stimulate production of serotonin in the brain which is a relaxant (Jensen 1994). This makes learners tired and lethargic. More information about food and the brain can be found in Chapter Eight.

Catering for Different Learning Styles in your Classroom

As 80 per cent of teachers tend to be visual learners, this learning style is often well catered for. School tends to be very visual – lots of reading, writing and showing. Tests and exams have a tendency to favour visual learners as they are most often written. It's the auditory and kinesthetic learners who can miss out in a visual classroom.

Your students will let you know how to cater for each learning style. When students start moving around and getting fidgety, this is a signal to you as the teacher, to allow students to move more. When students start talking more, use this as a signal to provide discussion time. I use a simple phrase, 'Please turn and discuss.' This quickly caters for both the auditory and kinesthetic learners. Invite your students to discuss the key points you have just covered or their opinions about an issue. You can use this phrase with every age group.

Catering for the olfactory and gustatory can be as simple as being aware of the smells in your classroom and allowing your students to have food more often. (Again, this will be discussed in more detail in Chapter Eight.)

It is also important to note that when introducing learning styles into your classroom you should clearly explain two points:

1. Every learner is all of these styles and will have one or two favourites. This does not of course mean that if they are visual, they can't learn auditorily. It's just not the best way for them to learn.

2. Encourage each student to take responsibility for their own learning style and ensure that the way they learn best doesn't interrupt someone else's learning style.

Chapter 2

Communicating with your Students

- VAK Communication

- Matcher and Mismatcher

- Impulsive and Reflective Learners

- Global and Analytical Learners

- Sequential and Random Learners

- Internally- and Externally-Referenced Learners

- Concrete and Abstract Learners

VAK Communication

Have you ever seen a blank look on the face of one of your learners when they appear to be confused? Ever heard learners mutter under their breath that they don't like the sound of what you're saying? Or have you ever had the feeling that your learners are just not receiving your message?

The words and phrases that you use can be the key to effective communication. The words you choose are also an indication of your own preferred learning style and a guide to recognising others' styles.

The simple phrase, 'I understand you' can be understood from three perspectives:

VISUAL: I see what you mean

AUDITORY: I hear what you're saying

KINESTHETIC: It feels right

> 'If children find learning difficult, it could well be that there is something the matter with the way we are asking them to learn, rather than something the matter with their innate capacity for learning.'
>
> **Frank Smith**

When people are communicating and not being understood, it is mis-communication, or cross-communication. One person may be using auditory words such as, 'You're not listening to me,' while the other is saying, 'You don't feel the same way as I do' (kinesthetic). They are both saying the same thing but using different language. For example, a father–daughter conversation about homework:

'Oh, I don't *see* why I have to do homework every night of the week.'

'*Listen*, you're starting to *grate* on me, you're *getting on* my nerves! How many times do I have to *tell* you to *do* your homework?'

'Oh, can't you *see*, I just want to *watch* this TV program for a few minutes more!'

We frequently communicate in the mode that suits us best, which is usually our dominant learning style. If you tune into the language other people use and match it, they instantly feel understood. It's a great way to build rapport with learners and parents. It is very subtle and highly effective.

When communicating to a class you can guarantee that all three learning styles will be in the room. One way to ensure you are reaching every learning style is to use a variety of questions that cover each of the three styles. Ask your students if they have *seen*, *heard* or had any *feelings* about your topic.

The following table lists visual, auditory and kinesthetic words. I constantly have this list close to hand to remind myself of other words and phrases I can use.

Visual Learners	Auditory Learners	Kinesthetic Learners
I see what you mean	I'm all ears	It feels right
Looks good to me	Sounds great to me	I've got a hunch
Picture this ...	That rings a bell	Hang in there
She is very colourful	To tell the truth	Get a grip on it
I'll see to it	That's unheard of	Pull some strings
That was clear cut	Tuned in/tuned out	Touch base
Appears to me	Give me your ear	Get a load of this
Bird's eye view	Loud and clear	Start from scratch

The following is a summary of other learner types you may experience in your classroom. Examples of each learner type are the extreme case. Each of us is a mixture of these and can change depending upon the circumstances.

Matcher and Mismatcher

Matcher students are those who learn by either matching things around them or finding similarities. These students search for patterns in new information and like consistency. A matcher will relate new experiences with past experiences and notice the similarities between the events.

Mismatcher students are those who find all the differences – what's missing, what's wrong or what's inconsistent. A common phrase may be, 'Yes I understand the pattern but …' Mismatchers will notice what was different about a new experience or event compared to a past event such as a school tour or a show they attended. They almost instantly notice when you have had a haircut, are wearing new shoes, have a button missing or have spelt a word wrong!

Mismatchers are often viewed as the challenging students. They tend to disagree with what the teacher says and can always come up with another way. These are the students who, when asked to use crayons, want to know if they can use markers … or when you say there are two ways to do a task, will come up with a third.

Matcher Characteristics

- cooperative
- find likenesses
- appear more polite
- like to please
- stay within the rules

Mismatcher Characteristics

- often appear disobedient

- see differences

- find other ways to do tasks

- notice mistakes

- like to compare and contrast

Try this activity to find out whether you are more likely to be a matcher or a mismatcher. We all have both within us and often have one dominant style.

What do you see?

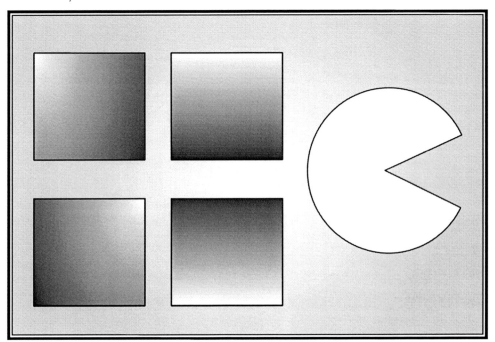

A matcher may see four squares and a pac man or an enzyme from the washing powder. A mismatcher may see squares with different thicknesses of lines or different shadings and a circle with a piece missing or may even notice that the lines don't quite match up.

Did you see something different? Were you focusing on the similarities or the differences?

Communicating in the Classroom

Matchers follow commands easily. They like routines and a predictability about their learning. They often want to know why you haven't started maths yet because it is past that time. They don't cope as well with a change of teacher or routine. Allow these students the opportunity to relate current learning to previous learning. Encourage them to seek firstly the patterns and sameness, and then the differences.

Mismatcher students have a tendency not to take commands or directions easily and often answer 'no' to a question, even if they mean yes. For example, when asking a mismatcher to please go and get the scissors, they may say no, because they were given a direction. However, they respond well to choice and questions such as, 'I wonder if there are enough scissors for everyone to use?' Because they like to find the differences and are curious they will be keen to find out if there are enough. Giving these students choice is also good, e.g. 'Would you like to do it before or after lunch?'

Obviously mismatcher students need to learn to take commands and directions because not everyone they meet will be aware of their learning style. So, after asking the question or giving the choice and when they are on their way to completing the task add, 'Great, please go and get the scissors,' or 'Super, we'll finish your spelling after lunch.' This will allow them to get more used to direct communication.

> Today's preparation determines tomorrow's achievement.

It's important to note that often a student will be a matcher at school and a mismatcher at home. This is one of the reasons parents say, 'Kayla's not like that at home.'

Impulsive and Reflective Learners

Impulsive learners act on impulse, often well before they think. They are the learners who have raised their hand to answer a question before you have asked it. They often call out answers, simply because they want to share. They respond before they think. These are the learners who, when you say, 'We're going outside for PE', are outside before you've told them exactly where to go!

Reflective learners need time to think about what they want to say or do. They often spend time weighing up all the facts before answering even a simple question. These are the learners who, three days after a topic, want to discuss it because they've now had time to reflect on it and come up with some conclusions.

Impulsive Characteristics

■ start tasks without all the instructions

■ like quick fire quizzes

■ call out answers often

■ raise hand and shake it (pick me, pick me …)

■ finish work quickly with little attention to detail

Reflective Characteristics

■ appear to be day dreaming

■ are often lost in thought

■ have a tendency to be quiet

■ pause before answering a question

■ need time to complete work

■ work is detailed

■ often good observers

■ start writing in the last five minutes of the time frame

Communicating in the Classroom

Ask the impulsives to do demonstrations – if you don't ask, they'll demonstrate anyway. The phrase, 'In a moment but not quite yet' is excellent to keep the impulsives still while giving instructions.

During questioning allow time for the reflectives to think about their answers. I modelled a technique developed by a Canadian lecturer:

Explain to the class that you're going to have a question time about (your topic): invite the learners who want to answer the questions straight away to sit in a certain place, and ask the learners who wish to think about their answers to sit in another area of the classroom. Have a list of the questions photocopied or written on the board for the reflectives to think about. Give them the questions and leave them to think. Now ask the other group the questions and get their answers straight away. When you have finished with the impulsive group either ask them to discuss the answers or begin a related task. Never leave impulsive learners with nothing to do – they will find something and it may not be what you had in mind! Go back to the reflective group and discuss their answers.

> 'Education is not filling a vessel but lighting a fire.'
>
> **Carl Jung**

You may notice learners one day deciding to be reflective and another to be impulsive. It often depends on how much they know about a topic, how they feel on the day, or even which group their friends are in. Many learners keep swapping groups to start with, but after a while settle into the group they prefer, once they realise it doesn't matter which one they choose.

NOTE: A handy rule of thumb when communicating with any student is to give them 10–12 seconds to respond. Often, as teachers, we jump in and answer for them or keep prompting them. If you wait, you'll find your learners may offer thoughts and comments that astound you.

> The rate at which you learn will become the only sustainable competitive advantage you'll have in your life.

Global and Analytical Learners

Global learners need the big picture. They like to see where concepts interrelate with other concepts and how it all applies to them. These learners need an overview of a topic first and tend to get frustrated with fine detail. They are good at multi-tasking and like to know the theme and purpose of a lesson first.

An analytical learner is able to process the details independently from each other. This learner loves details, facts and figures.

Global Characteristics

- need all the information before beginning

- want to know all the steps involved

- like to know what the finished product will be like

- need to know where the information fits into their own life

Analytical Characteristics

- like small chunks

- love facts and figures

- like to know all the fine details

- self-evaluate

- like step by step

- take a more logical approach

When doing a jigsaw puzzle an analytical learner will tend to take any two pieces and see if they fit together, then take another piece and so on. They also tend to start anywhere with the puzzle, and do sections as the pieces turn up. The global learner, after completing the frame, will compare a piece of the puzzle with the picture on the box and place it in the corresponding area within the frame.

Communicating in the Classroom

According to the Dunn & Dunn research, 70 per cent of teachers teach analytically and 70 per cent of students learn globally. The technique of hiding the page on an OHP and revealing it line by line (intellectual flashing!) drives a person who prefers to process globally insane. They want to see the whole thing so they can work out how it fits together.

Maths teachers tend to be analytical and might say, 'Today we are doing quadratic equations. Please turn to page 39 and complete numbers 1–5.' This, again, is frustrating for global processors as they are wondering, 'Given that we are all going to die, what is the point of quadratic equations?'. They need to be given a reason for learning them and how they will apply to their lives.

Analytical learners get very frustrated when teachers do not give any facts or figures. They often want to know, 'Who said?' and they respond to phrases such as 'research suggests …' or 'scientists have found …'. Their eyes often light up when the teacher mentions numbers and dates and they'll often write these down immediately.

Sequential and Random Learners

Sequential learners learn step by step. They want to know what comes first and they then add further information in steps. They like to know what's coming up next and they prefer to stay focused on a single task. Maths is a sequential subject where learners need each step in order, for example, you can't learn to multiply before you have learned addition. Multiplication is repeated addition.

> Forced silence and inactivity impair learners' choice for input and processing.

A random learner thinks chaotically and may have several projects going at once. During discussion there is often no apparent logical thought process as they jump from one point to another and you as the listener are left wondering how they went from topic A to topic X and back to topic G.

Sequential Characteristics

■ like step by step

■ more likely to read instructions first

■ tidy – everything has its place

■ often methodical

■ strong chronological narrative

■ one-task focused

Random Characteristics

■ like variety

■ have many tasks happening simultaneously

■ often wander off on a tangent when talking or writing

Communicating in the Classroom

Allow sequential learners to finish one task before going on to the next and give them the 'what's next?'. It's good to display your long term plans for these learners so they know where they're headed.

> The more I learn, the easier it gets.

Random learners will be very happy to have several projects on the go at the same time, however, they can be frustrated by being forced to do one task at a time. Allow these learners to work on contract so they can complete each day's tasks in the order they prefer.

> Education is what survives when what has been learned has been forgotten.
>
> **B.F. Skinner**

Internally- and Externally-Referenced Learners

Internally referenced learners operate from the way they think and feel and are not usually concerned about what others think of them. They often have their own set of rules and like to be independent from the norm. They are driven from an internal source.

Externally referenced learners are concerned about what others think. They may act according to how they perceive others want them to act or answer questions with the answers they think you want.

Communicating in the Classroom

Internally referenced learners do not respond to external rewards, usually only to a level they had indicated to themselves. These learners are independent thinkers so allow them to set their own goals and targets.

> Our aim is still for our school to be the best ... a school where all children leave school having identified a talent, a skill, an intelligence through which they can become whatever they want to be.
>
> **Michael Alexander**

Externally referenced learners respond well to external rewards such as praise and stickers. These learners often complete tasks to please the teacher.

Concrete and Abstract Learners

Concrete learners need concepts and examples that are real. They require hands-on experience, or something they can relate to. A common phrase from a concrete learner is, 'Give me an example.'

Abstract learners can cope with ideas and concepts without examples. Maths is an abstract subject, as is playing chess and learning a new language. The abstract learner enjoys talking and thinking as opposed to doing.

Communicating in the Classroom

Provide hands-on examples for the concrete learners. Frequently give real-life examples and stories so they can process this information. Be aware that abstract learners may not be enthusiastic about hands-on activities, preferring to think and hypothesise about the outcomes.

Chapter 3

Learning Environments

- Colour

- Lights

- Temperature

- Plants

- Music or Silence

- Food and Water

- Structure

- Social Environment

chapter 3

The physical environment in your classroom is an important factor in helping students to learn effectively. Small and often subtle changes can make a huge difference to your effectiveness and to your student's learning.

Colour

Use plenty of colour in your presentations and encourage your students to use colour in their work. This will increase their ability to remember and recall information. Research suggests that colour is processed near the part of the brain that stores long term memory. Information in colour is therefore more likely to be remembered. Traditionally, students have used blue or black. One colour is monotone – monotonous or boring for the brain. Using many colours is therefore more stimulating.

Encourage your students to use their favourite colours when taking notes, to highlight key information and to use markers of different thicknesses to make note-taking more fun. Use coloured handouts, colourful posters and colourful overhead transparencies.

 Teaching Ideas

Paint your classroom in bright warm colours.

◆◆◆

Use bright-coloured paper as backing to artwork rather than traditional black.

◉◉◉

Use a minimum of two colours when presenting information on the board.

☺☺☺

Turn your classroom lights off and see if the students notice.

■■■

Have the students who prefer bright light sit by the window.

It is better for students if your classroom temperature is 10 degrees too cold rather than 10 degrees too hot.

Place plants in the corners of your classroom or on shelves to increase oxygen in your room.

The colour of your classroom, as well as your clothes, can also have an impact on your students' moods and learning. Calming colours include light blue and light green. For optimal learning, colours such as beige, yellow or off-white are best. Research by Dr Harry Wohlfarth (1984) showed that painting the classroom walls in bright warm colours such as yellow and orange increased academic achievement. It also showed that students were less stressed, quieter, less moody and most impressively, that they were absent due to illness only one-third as often as students in a classroom with darker, cooler colours.

Lights

Research by Rita and Kenneth Dunn (1978) suggests that 70 per cent of students learn best with low lighting. Do you remember reading under the bed covers?

You didn't ruin your eyesight (as you were warned by your parents) because young children have excellent night vision. In fact, it's as we get older (from our mid-twenties) that the eye muscles begin to weaken and we need brighter light.

Bright light reflecting off a white page can stress the eyes and make learning harder. If possible avoid learning and teaching under fluorescent lighting as these lights flicker and cause tiredness, lack of motivation and sometimes headaches.

Turn your lights off in the classroom and wait to see if any of your students notice. Students who have a low light need will automatically do things to compensate in a high light environment. These include wearing a peaked cap, holding a book slightly inwards to shield the light and sitting in a dark corner or under a desk to read, think and work.

> Children can learn almost anything if they are dancing, tasting, touching, hearing, seeing and feeling information.
>
> **Jean Houston**

Temperature

Children have different temperature needs to adults. A popular quote in the accelerating learning field is, 'A jumper is something my mother makes me wear when she's cold!'. The ideal temperature for learning is 19° C. If students are too hot they are likely to fall asleep. During the winter, ensure there is fresh air available and your classroom isn't too hot. Girls often prefer to be one or two degrees warmer than boys.

Plants

Having plants in your learning environment not only brings the outdoors inside, but also provides a useful oxygen enhancer for the brain. NASA completed a study to determine which plants would be useful in a space shuttle for the best oxygen exchange (Underwood 1995). Four of the most common plants are the peace lily (this one is also great if you're not good at remembering to water plants), chrysanthemum, poinsettia (watch the leaves as they are poisonous) and ivy.

Music or Silence

Some of your students will prefer to work in silence, but it can be relatively difficult to find quiet spaces in our busy world. One of the easiest ways to achieve complete silence is to wear a pair of earmuffs – such as the ones you mow the lawn with – earplugs, or use some old headphones from the listening post. This is a very effective and rather unique way of finding quiet space.

For the students who prefer music in the background of their learning, the type you play can make a difference.

Teaching Ideas

Tape single tracks that you frequently use and need to access quickly onto 10-minute tapes with the same track on each side. This eliminates trying to find the track and having to rewind it.

■■■

Colour-code your tapes so they are easy to find in a hurry, for example red for discussion, purple for baroque, green for call-in songs and so on.

♫♫♫

Keep your tapes in a fabric tape holder without the covers so you can find the one you want quickly.

☺☺☺

It is important to have times with and without music, as music may annoy some of your learners.

♦♦♦

Ensure the music doesn't overshadow anything else – keep it softly in the background.

❖❖❖

Always push out the top tabs so a student can't accidentally tape over your music. I learned this the hard way!

❀❀❀

If the tape recorder chews your tape, stay calm and turn your iron to the lowest setting. Run the crinkled tape across the top of the iron and hey presto – good as new. Be careful not to have the iron too hot!

●●●

Provide a time when your students can play their own music – maybe two or three minutes before the lunch bell. I do advise, however, that you screen their music first – some is not appropriate for the classroom.

First, music without words is best. The brain is designed to learn and will always focus on the words of a song rather than the content you are teaching.

Second, baroque music will enhance your students' learning and memory. This is because it has a steady, rhythmic beat helps relax the student into a calmer state for learning (Ward & Daley 1993). It has a predictability about it, as opposed to the classical and romantic eras of music which can be unpredictable and more stimulating for the mind and body.

Baroque music slows down brainwaves from beta waves, where the mind and body are very active and very busy, to alpha waves, where the mind and body are calm and relaxed, allowing the long-term memory to be activated. Learning then becomes easy and rapid. Baroque composers include Pachelbel, Vivaldi, Handel, Bach, Corelli and Telemann. Baroque music playing softly is best used in the background when your students are working quietly at tasks such as writing and reading.

> Over two-thirds of children have music playing inside their heads at all times.

A study was conducted at Stanford University, USA, to determine the effect music has on plants (Rose 1987). Three identical rooms were set up with plants. All plants were treated equally during the three-month study.

In the first room there was complete silence. The second room had loud rock music pumped in; the third, quiet Baroque. At the end of the three months the plants were compared.

In the room with silence the plants were normal and healthy. The plants in the rock music room were shrivelling and dying. Finally, the plants in the Baroque music room had flourished beyond expectations. But more than this. Researchers noticed an unusual phenomenon. The plants were growing towards the speakers. Now, I know students' brains are not like plants … or are they?

Music for the Classroom

Discussion: Playing music while students are talking can enhance their discussion. Play it softly in the background so it doesn't intrude on the discussion.

> 99.9 per cent of learning is unconscious.
>
> **Eric Jensen**

Examples: Kenny G and Gato Babien.

Call-In Song: A song to let students know it's time to get ready to start the class. Very useful after morning recess and lunch and especially good for between classes as a guide for children to know how long they have to get to the next class.

Examples: 'Simply the Best', Tina Turner; 'Celebration', Kool and the Gang; 'Surfin' Safari', Beach Boys; Theme from *Friends*; 'No Limits', Hits Unlimited S2; 'Joy to the World', Three Dog Night; 'Life', Haddaway.

Special Effects: To add more fun into your program.

Examples: *Twilight Zone* theme; *Chariots of Fire*, Vangelis; 'Eye of the Tiger', Survivor.

Pack Up: A track of music that you can use at pack-up time so students know when to start packing up and how long they have. This music has a fast beat which indicates to pack up quickly.

Examples: *William Tell Overture*, Rossini; 'Heigh Ho Heigh Ho', from *Snow White and the Seven Dwarves*; *1812 Overture*, Tchaikovsky; 'Greased Lightning', *Grease* soundtrack.

Reflection: Useful to calm students and for stimulating creativity.

> **Examples:** 'The Mariner', Tony O'Connor; 'The Butterfly', Jeff Clarkson; Enya.

Baroque: Great for opening the brain to a receptive state of learning and accessing long term memory.

> **Examples:** Pachelbel, Corelli, Vivaldi, Telemann, Handel, Scarlatti, Bach.

Food and Water

I will discuss the value of adequate nutrition and water to personal performance in Chapter Eight, but it is important to also mention it here in the context of learning environments. There are strong links between efficient learning and good nutrition, so providing opportunities for your students to eat and drink at regular intervals throughout the day is essential.

Structure

Some students prefer to sit at a desk and chair, while others learn best lying on the floor or relaxed with their feet up on the sofa. Allow students to choose a place that is best for them. Some may even choose to walk around while thinking, or like myself, read while on an exercycle.

Social Environment

The social environment in your classroom is about the interactions between students and their interpersonal skills. Where is this set? In the staff room. It starts with YOU. In schools, we expect students to be respectful, responsible and caring. Are the teachers in your staff room? Are you?

> School should be the best party in town.
>
> **Peter Kline**

You are a role model in everything you do, even out of the students' eyes. Do you practise integrity with your teachings? If you expect students to be respectful, are you? If you want to instil the love of learning, do you love learning, are you learning new skills each week?

I learned this lesson when on a seven-day residential workshop for teenagers many years ago. After the first three days, I hadn't received any of the written warm fuzzies that all the other staff members had been sending and receiving, the little notes to tell you that you'd done a great job etc. I suddenly realised that I hadn't sent any. Zig Ziglar, the world's 'greatest salesman', says, 'You can have anything you want in your life. You just have to help enough people get what they want.'

Emerson says, 'What you do speaks so loud, we can't hear what you're saying.'

Your actions are more powerful than your words.

Chapter 4

Memory

- The Brain

- The Seven Keys to Memory

- Internal Processing

- Memory in the Classroom

- Memory and Spelling

Chapter 4

The Brain

How much do we know about how this amazing organ works? Imagine if you were given a car, the keys and some petrol, but you had no idea what to do with them. You might put the keys in the petrol tank and pour the petrol over the roof! Up until now this is how you may have used your brain because over 95 per cent of the world's knowledge about the brain has only been discovered over the past ten to twenty years.

Now is an exciting time to be living as far as our brain potential is concerned. For the first time in the history of the universe, brain researchers are discovering how to communicate effectively to the brain. What are the best ways to learn and study for the brain? How can you remember concepts and content easily?

Teaching Ideas

Teach your important information at the start of your lesson.

❖ ❖ ❖

Give students an outline of your lesson and the learning outcome at the start so they know what to expect and what to achieve.

ooo

Recap the important points of your lesson at the end.

✦ ✦ ✦

Teach for approximately 20 minutes and take a small break to allow for more firsts and lasts.

© 2004 Hawker Brownlow Education EIR3526

The Seven Keys to Memory

Primacy

Do you remember your first day of school? Your first time skating? What were you wearing and who did you talk to that day? What about your first kiss? Or the first time you drove a car? Do you remember your 47th day at school or the 11th kiss? Probably not, as these aren't as memorable as the first. In general, learners will recall and remember the first time they do something. Experience as many firsts as you can. Learners will also recall the beginnings of lessons or study times, so teach your key information at the start. Tell students what they are going to learn in the lesson at the beginning so they have a reason to participate in your lesson.

Recency

Which part of a movie is most remembered? Usually the ending. What about a novel? Again, it is most often the end that the reader remembers. The same is true of learning and teaching. By placing important or key information at the end of a lesson or the day, learners are more likely to remember it. Keep your lessons short as this allows for more firsts and lasts. I work on 20-minute intervals in my teaching, providing a break or discussion time for about 1 to 3 minutes before I continue with more content. Also, recap what students have learned during the lesson at the end so they leave your lesson with this information on top of their memory.

Repetition

Reviewing or periodic revision of material is needed to reactivate the stored memory and prevent it from being buried under other information. The more recent, regular and fun the review is, the easier it is to recall information.

Information can be reviewed visually by reading it, mind-mapping or highlighting; auditorily by discussing the key points; and kinesthetically (playing games). There are many games that can be adapted to provide rapid, fun reviewing of a topic, from simple card and board games to involved game shows.

A common schedule for repetition is one day, one week, one month and six months. Research suggests that when content is reviewed within 24 hours of first learning it, recall stays at around 90 per cent. If, however, the information is not reviewed for 72 hours (three days), recall drops to 30 per cent. Review yesterday's and last week's lesson content daily. It may only take two minutes and will reinforce the learning and memory for your students.

Stands Out

Anything that is funny, different or has a novelty value will stand out in your mind. Any 'one offs' will be memorable. Often, the sillier it is, the more memorable it will be. I have strong memories of a teacher who stood on his chair while teaching about height. The same teacher sat under a desk while teaching about earthquakes!

Using stories and analogies helps to make information stand out. Ensure your stories are relevant to your audience and have a fun or interesting element.

Mnemonics are also a fabulous way to make information stand out – such as learning to spell arithmetic (A Red Indian Thought He Might Eat Toffee In Church) or learning the periodic table in chemistry (How He Likes Beer By the Cup Full Not Over Frothy). (See examples on page 44.)

Chunking

Have you ever heard the saying, 'How do you eat an elephant? One bite at a time.'? According to David Sousa in 2002, the adult short-term memory can remember up to seven (plus or minus two) bits of information in one chunk. For teenagers this drops to five, plus or minus two; and for young children, three plus or

> How do you eat an elephant?
> *One bite at a time.*

minus two. When the brain is given too many pieces of information to remember, it installs amnesia. For example, read the following sequence of numbers, out loud to yourself, once, then turn away and write them down.

4, 12, 76, 21, 23, 19, 3, 67, 21, 88, 94, 5, 10

Did you feel your brain go fuzzy? This is what happens to the brain when teaching or learning too much information at once. Do you remember the first number? The last? Which one was repeated? These are the easiest to remember.

When remembering a telephone number, we often break it into smaller chunks to remember it. The smaller and more manageable the chunks, the faster learners will pick up and learn the information. Break your learning content into small pieces so it is easy to recall.

Association

Research suggests that when learning new information, if you link it to previous knowledge, recall is greatly improved. Thinking about 'concrete' or 'real-life' examples that students can relate to is useful. For example, when teaching the three parts of an essay, I've seen a teacher link or associate this information to a hamburger. The top bun is the introduction, the meat is

> I have an incredible memory …
> as long as I remember to use it.
>
> **Rich Allen**

the body of the essay (the more filling the better the hamburger – and the essay) and the bottom bun is the conclusion or summary. If you miss out one part you don't have a hamburger or an essay.

Take time to provide an overview of the key concepts at the beginning of a lesson or study time so that learners can hook learning to these as you learn. Metaphors are a way to associate information. Get your students to make some up. Example: How is maths like gardening?

Visuals

Visual recall is one of the fastest recalls the brain has. Pictures are located in the same area of the brain as the long term memory. Turn your concepts into pictures. The first picture you draw or think of is always the most memorable (primacy) and the sillier the picture the better (stands out). The more colourful the pictures, often the easier to remember. Visuals can be imagined, drawn or made. If pictures are not an option such as with dates or some words in another language, write them big and in colour. The brain will process this as a picture not a word.

Internal Processing

It has long been said that the eyes are the windows to the soul. Only recently have researchers learned how true this is. Simply by observing a person's eyes, you can immediately see which representational system – visual, auditory or kinesthetic – they are using at that specific time (Knight 1995). As people represent information internally, they move their eyes, even if only slightly.

Answer these questions, or ask another person and watch their eyes:

■ How many windows are there in your house? Take a moment to remember. To answer that question 90 per cent of people will look up and to the left as they are recalling a visual image of their house.

■ What would you look like if you had green hair? This time your eyes probably went up to the right, as this is where people's eyes go to access constructed images. (That's if you don't have a picture of yourself with green hair already stored in your memory!)

By watching people's eyes it is possible to know which sensory mode they are processing in. To access what we have heard we tend to look sideways, we look to the left for remembering, and to the right for constructing a new thought. When we look down to the left, this is our self-talk channel – that little voice inside your head that talks to you telling you how amazing you are, or not!

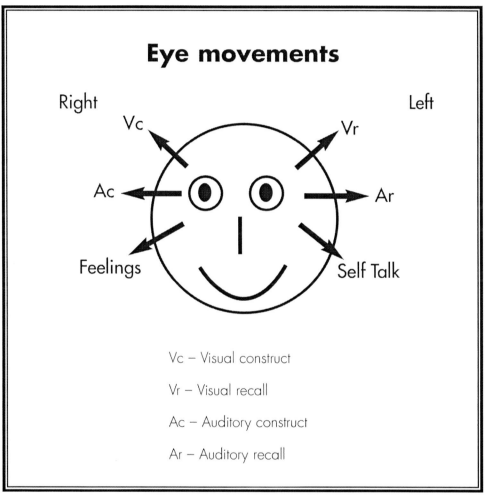

Eye movements

Right   Left

Vc   Vr

Ac   Ar

Feelings   Self Talk

Vc – Visual construct

Vr – Visual recall

Ac – Auditory construct

Ar – Auditory recall

Looking down to the right accesses our feelings channel. It is important to note that about 5 per cent of the population is reversed from this model, so to remember they look to the right instead of the left.

Where do children – or adults for that matter – look when they are crying? Down, as they are accessing their feelings channel. When you ask a person who is crying to look up, they will stop crying. Why? When you look up you cannot access your feelings.

When trying to recall information it is useful to put your eyes in the direction of where that thought is stored. If you want to remember what you said a few days ago it would not be so useful to look down or up. The memory would be found quickest if you look sideways and to the left.

Some people look straight ahead to access information and often look like they have 'checked out'. They are looking inwards for the answers, seeing the pictures inside their head.

Visual processing is much faster at a neurological level than auditory or kinesthetic processing (Grinder 1991). Notice the picture on the page and in a moment close your eyes. Notice how long the actual picture lasts – not the reconstructed picture you make up, but the actual picture. For most people this picture disappears in a split second. Now clap your hands. Does that sound last for a longer or shorter period of time than the picture disappearing? Again, the majority of people find the sound lasts longer, indicating that it takes a longer time for the brain to process. Now squeeze your hand, or someone else's if available. Notice that this sensation lasts even longer than the sound.

Kinesthetic processing is much slower again. This doesn't suggest that kinesthetic learners are slow, merely that they may process and recall information at a slower rate than visual learners. It's almost like comparing a Ferrari with a Volkswagen. They both have their place, but put them on the race track and we know which one will win. The same goes for our visual, auditory and kinesthetic students. Put them in an exam room and we know which will be most likely to win. Visual students will, because of their speed of processing. Visual information is processed quickly, and when we look up we access our visual memory – combining these two makes for some powerful learning.

Memory in the Classroom

Place all your important information on the top left of your board or just above eye level in your classroom. This will allow the students to look up at it – therefore accessing the visual part of the brain.

Three weeks before a major topic, I would put the required prior knowledge in the form of pictures, posters and questions up high around my classroom walls. I would not draw attention to it, yet by the beginning of the topic the information seemed to have 'gone in' almost by a process of osmosis. The class had a

Teaching Spelling Visually

STEP 1

Write the word on a card in clear letters using the appropriate lower and upper case letters. Write each letter in a different colour to stimulate the memory.

water

STEP 2

Hold the card up high so your eyes are looking up, without the head moving up.

STEP 3

Take many snap shots of the word by blinking about 20 times. With younger students a buddy can hold the card up high and flash it in and out of sight. This makes many pictures in the brain. Ensure you only look. Resist saying the word or letters to yourself.

STEP 4

Close your eyes and look up – with your eyes still closed. Do you remember the colours?

STEP 5

With your eyes closed see the word in your head. Spell it backwards. Spell it forwards.

STEP 6

Open your eyes. Did you get it right? If yes, celebrate. If not, repeat the process from step 2.

knowledge of the majority of work to be covered and even understood some of the main concepts. This allowed me to teach at a deeper or wider level.

A friend of mine took this model and applied it in her year 1 class. As the children were just learning to read and spell she placed five basic spelling words on the top left of her whiteboard each week. Without teaching them, she found that 90–95 per cent of her class consistently knew how to spell those words the following week.

A secondary chemistry teacher has also used this to the advantage of her students. She wrote the chemical formulas of the precipitates on card in the colours of the precipitates and placed them above her whiteboard. She maintains the students do not have the difficulty past students had in remembering the formulas and colours.

Memory and Spelling

Watch any good speller and you'll see that they look up to spell a word – it's natural. Spelling in the English language is a visual skill, not an auditory skill as many of us have been taught. Many words in English do not look as they sound. For example: enuf, nif, nite, encarijd and so on.

If spelling in English is a visual skill, how then can we teach it visually? We need to encourage learners to see the word rather than sound it out. The process of teaching spelling visually is shown on page 49.

This same process can be used for learning maths and science formulas, history dates or any information that requires fast recall. In fact, when you are good at this process, it can be used to recall pages of text. With young children, start with three pictures, then three letters in a random order. Finally, use three letter words such as 'cat'. Remember it is easier for young children to spell words that have personal concrete meaning.

When teaching the visual spelling process to

younger children, start with three symbols,

then move to random letters

and finally, words.

Chapter 5

Motivation and Mistakes

Chapter 5

- Affirmations

- Physiology

- Making Mistakes

- Four Levels of Learning

- Motivation and Rewards

A question I often get asked is, 'Is motivation permanent?'. I'd have to answer no, but neither is cleaning. It's something we have to keep doing and doing and doing. In this chapter we'll look at how to keep yourself and your students motivated and the importance of making mistakes. I believe that all humans have the same ability to achieve success and the one big difference that affects the degree of success is an individual's belief system – what we believe of our own ability. This is the first key to motivation.

The subconscious mind is one of the most powerful instruments in the universe. It cannot tell the difference between fact and fiction. It will believe anything you or someone else tells it (Kehoe 1994).

> People who say it cannot be done should not interrupt those who are doing it.

For a demonstration on how this works, complete the activity below with another person:

ACTIVITY

Ask your partner to hold their arm out at shoulder height. Apply downwards pressure on their wrist. Be firm and gentle. Now ask your partner to say out loud, 'I am strong, I am strong, I am strong.' Again, place pressure downwards on the wrist and notice the difference. Now ask your partner to say out loud, 'I am weak, I am weak, I am weak,' and place downward pressure on the wrist. Notice this time that the arm may be easier to push down. Finally repeat 'I am strong' and test the resistance.

Note: It is important to leave them at strong.

Notice how even if your partner doesn't believe they are weak, their arm goes down with less pressure. It's the subconscious brain believing what it has been told – in this case, weak or strong.

You have patterning in you like this for many things, such as your beliefs about your abilities, your strengths and your weaknesses. The more times you hear or say something to yourself the more likely you are to remember it and believe it.

Affirmations

One way to change this patterning is by using affirmations. These are positive phrases you repeat over and over to yourself. There are four guidelines to writing affirmations:

1. An affirmation must start with the word 'I', 'my' or your name. This is so your brain knows you are talking about yourself and not someone else. Often people talk from the position of 'you' which means they are separating themselves from the event. For example, when someone says, 'You know when you do something silly and everyone looks at you?', they usually mean, 'I did something silly and everyone looked at me.'

2. Affirmations work best when they are positive. This means that you avoid the words 'not', 'don't' and 'when'. For example, 'I'm not going to fail maths,' reinforces the word 'fail' rather than the word 'pass'. You should say, 'I pass exams easily.'

3. Affirmations work best if they are in the present tense as though they are true already – telling the truth in advance. Use phrases such as 'I am', 'I have' and 'I enjoy'. Phrases such as 'I will' are in the future tense. These tell your brain that it will happen in the future. Interesting concept – tomorrow is in the future and tomorrow never comes. It's always today. I hear people in their lives saying phrases such as, 'I will be happy when I leave school … I will be happy when I get a job … I will be happy when I get married … I will be happy when I have children … I will be happy when the children leave home…' and these people forget to be happy right now!

4. You must take ACTION. Positive thinking alone doesn't work if you sit on the couch all day saying, 'I'm getting fit. I'm fit and energetic.' Unless you take some positive action, it won't happen.

Sample Affirmations

As you read through this list, notice what that little voice says inside your head. Your response is a reflection of your beliefs.

I pass my exams easily and effortlessly.

I am an energetic teacher.

I am an organised person.

I am a super netball player.

I speak clearly and precisely.

I have a fantastic memory.

I have an abundance of money.

I am great at maths.

I can draw well.

My life is perfect and all my needs are met.

My relationships get stronger and stronger each day.

I deserve good things.

I am healthy and happy.

I remember easily.

I spend quality time with those I love.

I am creative.

I enjoy the students I work with.

I love my job.

I love life.

I am calm and relaxed.

I spend quality time for myself daily.

Research suggests that you need to say an affirmation approximately twenty times a day for twenty days to re-pattern your mind (Robbins 1991). The way this works is that in your brain is a part called the reticular activating system (RAS), the purpose of which is to wake up the brain for incoming stimulus. Have you ever been in a room full of people and heard your name mentioned over the other side of the room? Or when you've just bought a new car, you suddenly notice all the other cars on the road that are the same as yours and the same colour? This is your RAS working. When you use affirmations it wakes up the RAS to look for all the reasons you do have a fantastic memory (if this is your affirmation, for example) rather than what it may have been doing, searching for all the reasons why your memory is bad.

Your brain is designed to learn and will search and search for an answer when a question is asked. The quality of the questions you ask your students is therefore very important. Are you asking a positive question for which their brain will seek a positive answer or are your questions negative?

Physiology

Communication is more than words. In fact, it is made up of three key components:

Words	7%
Tone	38%
Physiology	55%

It's not what you say but how you say it that counts. If a person is slouched in their chair and, talking in a slow monotone voice, says, 'I'm really excited about this new project,' the listener picks up the real message from the tone and physiology or body language, rather than from the words.

There is a big difference in my mother calling, 'Karen,' and 'KAREN!'. Same words, totally different meaning.

If I said to you, 'a very depressed person is about to walk into your home', how would you imagine this person to look, move, breathe and speak? What about a highly excited person? Both states are very different. How a person feels is reflected in their body movements or physiology.

Paying attention to how you move your body and how you feel means that you can use this information at a conscious level. Notice how you move your hands, how quickly you speak and where you look (eye contact or not) when you are speaking about something you love, perhaps a hobby or fun recreational activity. Notice how you use your body when speaking about a boring topic.

One way to change how you feel about a situation is to simply change your physiology. If you're feeling down, sit up, smile and breathe deeply. You are guaranteed to feel better.

Paying attention to how you move your body and how you feel will also help keep your students interested in the topic and motivated to learn. If the students are getting restless, check your physiology first, then get them to change theirs.

A positive physiology promotes an increase in blood flow and therefore more oxygen to the brain, which enhances learning.

Nine Simple Ways to Change the Physiology of your Students

- Ask students to 'turn and discuss' the information you have just presented.

- Get students to stand up and do an activity.

- Do some mental fitness activities.

- Ask students to get a drink of water.

- Invite students to touch all four walls and find a new seat to sit in.

- Tell a joke.

- Take a deep breath.

- Change activities.

- Put some upbeat music on while they're completing activities.

Making Mistakes

Understanding the role of mistakes in learning is one of the keys to accelerating learning and keeping students motivated. Rather than being discouraged by errors, students should be taught to learn from their mistakes. Have you ever seen a baby learning to walk? They finally get themselves up on two feet, take that amazing first step forward and … fall.

> The reason I know so much is because I have made so many mistakes.
>
> **R. Buckminster Fuller**

Again, they pull themselves back up, step and fall. This is a natural process that continues until they can walk, then run.

At no point does the parent say, 'You have fallen over too many times. You'll never learn to walk.' It's a natural expectation that the child will walk, however long it takes.

So what about all other tasks? Reading, writing, maths, tying a shoelace, learning to ride a bike, rollerskating, driving a car or waterskiing. These processes are learned easily by the person who is not afraid of mistakes and is willing to learn from each mistake.

In his book *If You Want to Be Rich and Happy … Don't Go to School* Robert Kiyosaki says, 'Kids care more about their grades than what they could learn. Our education system rewards right answers and penalises mistakes. But what is really important are the wrong answers … It's not what you know that's important, it's what you don't know. Only when you find out something you don't know will you gain knowledge … Learning is a simple process of making mistakes, finding out what you don't know and correcting.'

When making movies a director will shoot as many 'takes' as necessary to get the best shot. Each time the scene is not correct the director calls it a mis-take and asks the crew to do it again a little differently. This is the major key to learning from mistakes. To recognise where you went wrong and correct it. A six year old once explained it to me as a maze. 'When you come to a dead end you go back and find out where you went wrong and take another path.'

In the classroom, discuss with your students the fact that mistakes are useful to learning. In fact, in my classroom we redefined mistakes and called them 'learning experiences'. This gave mistakes a more positive view allowing students to have fun and enjoy the learning process. After attending one of my workshops a school in Christchurch has produced stickers for children's work that say, 'Just Another Learning Experience'.

Four Levels of Learning

Maslow's Levels of Learning

Level 1: Unconscious Incompetency

When your students don't know that they don't know. For example, when they were little they didn't know that they didn't know how to tie a shoelace. They may not know that they don't know how to do quadratic equations.

Level 2: Conscious Incompetency

Your students know they don't know. That is, they know they don't know how to tie a shoelace or how to solve quadratic equations.

Level 3: Conscious Competency

Your students process each step individually. To tie a shoelace – left over right and under ... and pull ... Maths equations are worked out step by step, slowly and methodically.

Level 4: Unconscious Competency

Your students don't have to think about the process any more. They can perform the skill without thinking of the individual parts. So now, they can tie their shoelaces without thinking about how, and they can solve equations as fast as they know their times-tables.

Which level are your students at?

How do you know when your student has learned a new skill? Is it when the information is first taught? Or when the box on your checklist is ticked? Maybe after the information has been recalled during a test, or when your students can use and apply the information to real-life situations?

Learning is like making a track to the top of a bush-clad hill. The first time the path is difficult and confusing as you slash through the obstacles and come across natural barriers, all while you are maintaining your sense of balance and direction. The fourth time you begin to head for the top, the track is a little easier and you only have to shift debris and branches that have fallen on your path. Eventually, after 100 trips up the hill, your path is now a four-lane highway and your journey is relatively effortless, requiring little thought.

Reaching level 4 (see opposite), the level of unconscious competency, is when true learning has taken place. So how does a student get from level 1 to level 4? Practice, perseverance and encouragement. By making mistakes, learning from them and correcting them. Allow your students to go through these levels. Provide them with many opportunities for experimentation, practice and time to think about each step. Each student will work through the levels at their own rate.

Maslow says that it can take about three to four weeks of practice to move from one level to another. This of course depends on the quality and frequency of practice and any prior knowledge brought to the learning situation. Also, the more reason a student has to learn a new skill, the easier and faster it will be to master. Create interest and excitement about a topic by giving real practical applications so students are more focused on learning their new skill.

Motivation and Rewards

Eric Jensen, a world leader in accelerated learning and brain based research, suggests motivation, or lack of it, in our classrooms is often only temporary. He states, 'Students who make it to school each day already have some degree of motivation. Truly unmotivated students are still in bed, or any place other than school' (Jensen 1998).

Even if your students don't look like they want to be in your classroom, at least they have made it there. Most likely they are temporarily unmotivated. There are three primary reasons for this:

1. Students often bring negative associations and experiences from the past to new learning situations. Memories of negative experiences are stored in the mid brain area and when triggered can release chemicals such as adrenaline. A teacher's voice, gestures or tonality may remind a student of a teacher they disliked, triggering anxiety of the past.

Six key strategies to encourage students to uncover their intrinsic motivation

1. Eliminate threat. It takes time and a strong intent, but it's worth it. Ask students about the factors that inhibit their learning and correct them.

2. Goal setting with student choice on a daily basis can provide a more focussed attitude.

3. Influence positively in everything you do and say. Make your number one motive in teaching to help students feel good about themselves. This includes using affirmations, acknowledging success, using positive posters and teamwork.

4. Manage student emotions through the productive use of rituals, drama, movement and celebration. Teach students how to manage their own emotions, too.

5. Feedback. Set up learning so students get endless, self-managed feedback. Ideas for this include the use of computers, group work, checklists and peer editing.

6. Prepare students for a topic with 'teasers' or personal stories to spark their interest.

2. De-motivation can be environmental. The learning style of a student may not be met, especially that of auditory and kinesthetic learners, who need to talk and move around to learn best. Other de-motivating factors include room temperature, lighting, hunger, lack of resources, lack of respect (in both students and teachers), bad seating, language barriers, fear of failure and irrelevant lesson content.

3. The student's relationship with the future may be the cause of a lack of motivation. Students require clear, well defined, meaningful goals that they set and strive towards as well as a positive belief about themselves and learning. The latter is critical for motivation and success. Positive thinking engages the left frontal lobe of the brain and triggers the release of pleasure chemicals like dopamine and endorphines. This self reward reinforces the desired behaviour.

Dean Wittick, head of the Division of Educational Psychology at the University of California in Los Angeles, suggests that today's classroom teaching is based on a flawed theory. 'For a long time, we've assumed that children should get an immediate reward when they do something right. But the brain is much more complicated than most of our instruction; it has many systems operating on parallel' (Jensen 1998). The brain is perfectly satisfied to pursue novelty and curiosity, embrace relevance and bathe in feedback from successes. He suggests extended applications of projects and problem-solving where the process is more important than the answer. 'That's the real reward,' he says.

As teachers, our understanding of motivation has changed. Stickers, stamps, stars, coupons and gimmicks may no longer make sense when compared to the alternatives.

Neuroscientists have a different perspective on rewards. The brain makes its own rewards. They are called opiates, which are used to regulate stress and pain. The reward centre is based in the brain's centre. The pleasure-producing system lets you enjoy behaviour like affection, sex, entertainment, caring or achievement. It's a long-term survival mechanism. It's as if the brain says, 'That was good. Let's remember that and do it again.' Students who succeed usually feel good and that's reward enough for most of them.

> Commitment is the ability to get back up.

Teaching Ideas

Create opening and closing rituals in your classes. When students know exactly what to expect at the beginning and end of a class they feel safer and more comfortable about new learning.

◆◆◆

Be aware of and teach to the different learning and thinking styles.

Provide students with greater choice within the classroom.

☺☺☺

Eliminate any kind of embarrassment or use of sarcasm.

■■■

Provide real-life applications of curriculum content. Relate new learning to student's current knowledge.

✦✦✦

Provide more quantity, variety and quality of feedback.

◆◆◆

Encourage better nutrition so the brain has all it needs to maximise the learning potential.

So are external rewards also good for the brain? Neuroscientists say no (Jensen 1998). The brain's internal reward system varies between students. Most teachers have found that the same external reward can be received completely differently by two students. How students respond can depend on genetics, life experiences, individual brain chemicals and learning styles. Students who are under tremendous stress and pressure will have developed high levels of survival skills within the brain. For these students, their brains are not always rewarded by the satisfaction of completing their homework.

An effective reward needs to have two elements: predictability and market value (Jensen 1998). If students are unaware of the reward and receive it after the event, it's not a reward but a celebration. If given the option of 'Do it well, and you'll get a pizza' before the event, then it's a reward. Pizza, lollies, stickers, stars, privileges and certificates all have market value. However, research suggests that students will want them each time the behaviour is required; in fact, they'll want an increasingly valuable reward and rewards provide little or no lasting pleasure. Amabile (1989) has documented extensively how the use of rewards damages intrinsic motivation.

Is providing intrinsic motivation a key for teachers? One of them, suggests Eric Jensen. He states, 'Most students are already intrinsically motivated. It's just the motivation is very content dependent.' A student who is unmotivated in a traditional maths class can become excited and energetic when working out how to budget and spend their first pay cheque.

Chapter 6

Goal Setting
and Success

- Goal Setting

- The Cycle of Success

- Attitude

- Visualisation

- The Pygmalion Effect

- Words to Avoid when Aiming for
  Success

Chapter 6

Goal Setting

Specific

When setting goals, ensure they are specific. You get whatever you ask for from life. For example, a young girl working in the Spectrum office had her birthday while in employment with us. I was prepared to buy her a birthday gift but I was unsure what she might need, want or indeed what was appropriate. So I asked her. 'What would you like for your birthday?' She replied with, 'Dunno.' So I didn't buy her anything. She learned her lesson. Each time I asked her for information after this she told me what she wanted and received something in return. (Obviously if she had asked for something unrealistic she may not have received it, and being realistic is a part of goal setting.)

How can anyone give us what we want in life if we fail to tell them? When setting goals, be specific.

Measurable

How will you know when you have achieved a goal? Make them measurable so you can celebrate your success. Imagine running a marathon and not having a finish line. How would you know when you had finished?

A friend once set a goal to run a half marathon in 2 hours 22 minutes. She placed a card above the stove with this time. She ran the race and the stopwatch recorded her time as 2 hours 22 minutes.

Achievable

I asked my friend, 'What would have happened if you had set your goal at 2 hours 18 minutes?'. She replied that at the time, that was not so achievable. It is now!

Realistic

Is the goal realistic? Let's say I set a goal to swim The English Channel. Is it achievable? Yes, I have the ability to do this. And is it realistic? No, not while I travel throughout the country each week. When would I train? Being realistic means you are willing to do what it takes to achieve that goal.

Time Frame

Putting a date or time frame on your goals is important. When do you want to achieve it by? This year or next? Many people have set goals and left out this fifth step of time frame. They have met their goals many years later.

> Set goals and make your dreams come true.

In 1953, a survey of the graduating class at Harvard University revealed that only 3 per cent had set any form of written goals. Twenty years later, that same 3 per cent had more success, wealth and happiness than the other 97 per cent put together (Sugars 1998).

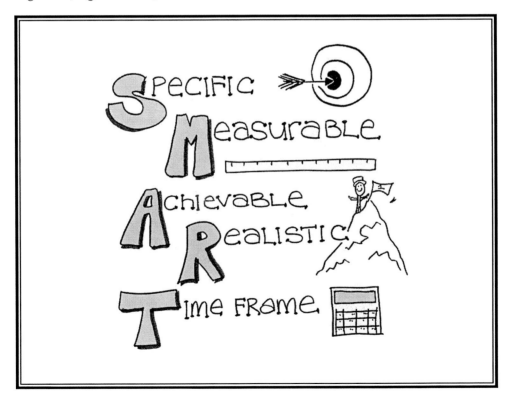

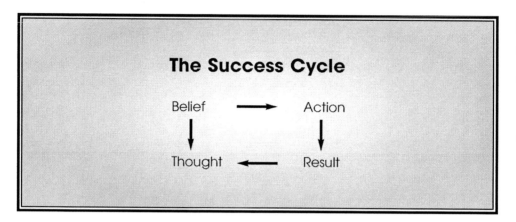

The Cycle of Success

Creating success over and over again is as simple as following the four areas of the success cycle. A simple idea that works with a little practice.

Belief

Your beliefs are a combination of your experiences and lessons since birth. They are a set of ideas about life that you hold true. We all operate our lives from a set of beliefs, and each person is different. You have beliefs about how long you will live, how much money you are worth and what is possible for you and your students.

Your beliefs affect your ability. For example, if a student believes they are bad at maths, then their potential for learning maths declines, and in turn ability drops. This is because the reticular activating system in the brain (mentioned earlier in Chapter 5) will prove your beliefs to you.

Action

The actions you take in your life depend on your beliefs. Let's say you want to change jobs and you see the perfect job description in the paper. The salary is €65,000. Next week you see exactly the same job. The only change now is the salary is €450,000. Would you still apply? Your beliefs about your own worth might start showing up. Without action very little is likely to happen. Action is both internal, such as thinking and planning, and external, such as practice and physical action. When you take action, sooner or later you will get a result.

Result

The results you get are feedback which reflect on your actions. You will not always get the results you desire. Life is a game and there will always be challenges. If your results are not what you expected, check your actions. If you are getting results then you are making useful actions.

Thought

Your thoughts are the key to achieving success. Let's look at an example to make this clearer.

Imagine you own a bright red sports car. Now, you have a *belief* that in Ireland and the U.K. it's OK to drive on the right hand side of the road. You take *action* according to this belief and drive on the right hand side of the road. Sooner, rather than later, you will get a *result* which is likely to be a crash.

Assuming you survive, you may blame the other drivers on the road, or you may make an excuse for why you drove like that, or you may even deny that there is a problem. These types of thoughts are the thinking of a 'victim'. On the other hand, you may choose to take ownership and responsibility for your result and change your belief, changing your action to achieve a different result. So now you decide it's best to drive in the middle of the road. And so the success cycle continues. There is no magic number of times you will spiral through the cycle, as we all learn at a different rate. It really depends on the quality of the thought. When successful people throughout the world get something wrong, or it doesn't go quite how they expect, they take responsibility for their results and correct their beliefs and actions until they reach the desired result or outcome.

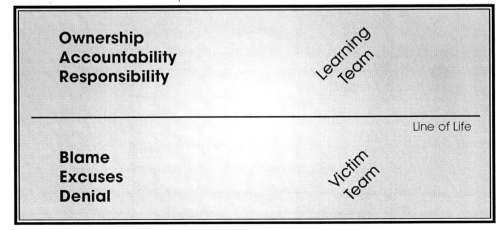

Ownership
Accountability
Responsibility

Learning Team

Line of Life

Blame
Excuses
Denial

Victim Team

As long as we are alive, we are spiralling up and down through the success cycle. Life cycles don't stand still. Keep things moving, choose actions and attitudes which increase your potential and watch the improved results.

Attitude

I find it fascinating that when asking someone how their day was, they reply with phrases such as 'not bad' or 'fine considering'. Is 'bad' the benchmark? What about replying 'outstanding, and I'm improving' or 'super good, and I'm getting better' as Zig Ziglar does. Even if you don't really feel like this, it's telling the truth in advance.

One way of maintaining a positive attitude is by always looking for the good in others and in all situations.

'Every day's a great day!' says my dad. 'Just try missing one.' We all have the choice to choose how we feel. Do you focus on the 80 per cent of your life that's going fantastically well, or the 20 per cent that isn't?

Visualisation

The power of such a simple tool as visualisation is immense. Napoleon Hill, author of *Think and Grow Rich*, said, 'What the mind can conceive and believe it will achieve.'

Many studies have proven this over and over again.

A Stanford University researcher took the three top basketball teams and asked them to throw basketballs from the free throw line. On average, players scored eight out of ten successful shots.

The teams then had a different task for the duration of the study. Team one were asked to go to the courts each day and practice throwing balls into the hoop from the free throw line. Team two were told not to go to the courts and not to practice. Team three's requirement for the study was to go to the courts each day and sit on the benches and visualise throwing the balls into the hoop.

At the end of the study, when players were asked to shoot ten baskets, team one averaged eight out of ten, team two averaged eight out of ten and team three scored ten out of ten. Why? One reason is that each time they practised they were successful. That is, every time they visualised practising they got the ball in. A 100 per cent success rate.

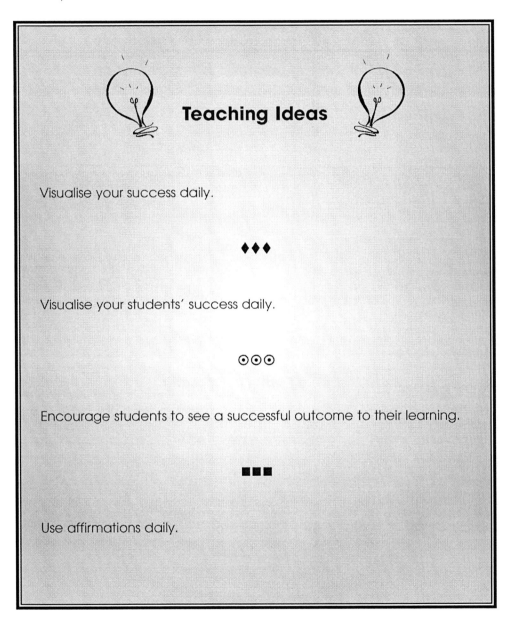

Teaching Ideas

Visualise your success daily.

◆◆◆

Visualise your students' success daily.

⊙⊙⊙

Encourage students to see a successful outcome to their learning.

■■■

Use affirmations daily.

How many of your students have seen themselves as successful? When Roy Disney, Walt Disney's brother, opened Euro-Disney in Paris a reporter remarked to him, 'What a shame Walt isn't here to see this.' Roy smiled and replied, 'You don't understand. He saw it, and that's why it's here.'

The Pygmalion Effect

The power of your own beliefs is an incredible force in your classroom. In his classic book, *Pygmalion in the Classroom*, Rosenthal shares an age old study. A teacher was told that a group of students were highly intelligent. In fact, the students had tested well below normal and often displayed behaviour problems.

> Where you put your *attention* is where you get your *results*.
>
> **Tony Robbins**

Unknowing, the teacher figured that if these were gifted students, then she'd better treat them that way. You can guess the end of the true story. The more she treated them that way, the more they responded that way. She literally created gifted students. This study, over forty years old, is one of the most astonishing accounts about the power you have over the success of your students and your own children.

What you believe, you will create ...

Words to Avoid when Aiming for Success

Don't

Don't think of yellow, don't think of a blue tree, don't think of ice-cream. Chances are that when you read those things you did think of them, even though I said not to. Why? Our brain is unable to recognise the word 'don't' (Laborde 1994). When you have a thought you create a picture, sound or feeling of it in your mind, then think not to do it.

For example, if you say to a child who is climbing a tree, 'Don't fall', the child has to create the picture, the sound or the feeling of themselves falling, then think not to. And what nearly always happens? The child falls out of the tree.

What should we say? Instead of saying what you don't want, tell the child what you do want. For example, 'Climb carefully' or 'Check the branch is strong before standing on it'.

Sounds easy? With so much of our conditioning around language it is a constant challenge to remember not to use that word, especially with so much advertising that says, 'Don't drink and drive' (instead of 'Drive sober') and the most common, 'Don't forget' (instead of 'Remember').

> The power of your mind is that you always have the ability to choose.

Try

Avoid using the word 'try'. If I asked you to try and pick up the pen I'd dropped on the floor and you picked it up, then you haven't tried, you've done it. If you left the pen on the floor, then you haven't picked it up. As Yoda, the Jedi master from *Star Wars* says, 'Try? There is no try. Either do or do not.'

Can't

How many of us remember saying 'I can't' as a child, only to be told by our parents, 'There's no such word as can't.' We know there is a word, it's just not a useful one. When you use the words 'I can't' they simply shut the mind down to other possibilities. Another way to think about those challenging situations is, 'How can I?'

I can't spell – How can I learn to spell?

I can't dance – What can I do in order to dance?

I can't afford it – What can I do to be able to purchase this?

Chapter 7

Mind Mapping and Speed Reading

- Mind Mapping

- Speed Reading

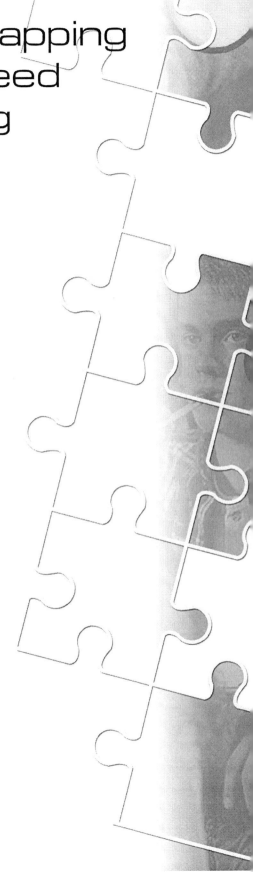

Chapter 7

Mind Mapping

Mind mapping is an essential skill for learning faster and retaining information. It is a brain-friendly way of taking notes. Mind mapping uses both the left logical and the right creative brain. It uses the memory key of association and reflects the way the brain naturally works (North & Buzan 1991).

Step One

Turn your page sideways, as this is the shape of your memory. Take a moment and close your eyes. Is the TV screen of your mind portrait or landscape? Yes, it's landscape, so if you turn your page it will reflect your memory recall. It is best if the paper is blank so you are not constricted by the lines.

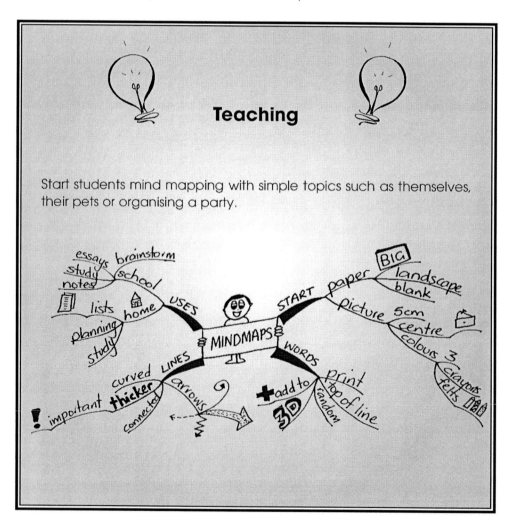

Teaching

Start students mind mapping with simple topics such as themselves, their pets or organising a party.

Step Two

Start in the centre – this is the focus of the mind map. Again, this is where your brain naturally starts. Close your eyes and see the blank TV screen. Now picture a red car on that screen. Where does your brain put it? For most people it will be in the middle. Start with a picture or visual image that is approximately 5 centimetres high and uses three colours. The colour stimulates your right creative brain and the picture opens up associations and focuses the thoughts.

Step Three

Add main themes, like chapter headings in a book. These words should be printed so they are easy to read. The words are placed on top of the line and the lines are the same length as the word. Central lines are thick and curved and should be thick in the centre, moving to thin. This mirrors the shape of a brain cell. Thicker lines show importance. Lines are connected to the central image.

Step Four

Add the second level of thought. These words are linked to the main branch that trigger them. Mind mapping is not like writing sentences. Key words branch from associated ideas and words.

Step Five

Add further levels of data and information. Use images as much as you can. Allow thoughts to come freely, meaning you can hop between ideas and themes.

Step Six

Add dimension, highlights, arrows, codes and visual images to make your mind map beautiful, artistic, colourful and imaginative.

Speed Reading

Have you ever found yourself reading the same line over and over again? Have you ever read to the bottom of the page and had no idea what you'd just read? This may be because you're reading too slowly.

We speak at an average rate of 250 words per minute. Our brains, however, are capable of reading much faster than this. If you're only reading at 250 wpm then your brain can get bored and start to think about other things, such as what you're going to have for dinner and activities for the weekend.

So how do you increase your reading speed? You simply follow several key principles.

1. Beliefs affect ability. If you believe you can read faster with excellent comprehension, then you can. If you don't believe you can, you won't.

2. Use your finger to guide your eyes. Your eyes often tend to be lazy and will flick all over the page when reading. Push your eyes faster by running your finger under the words you are reading to keep your eyes focused and on track.

3. Read with a purpose. Decide on your purpose for reading something before reading it. Do you want an overview, the facts, the details? Are you looking for the answer to a specific question or are you just reading for enjoyment?

4. Practise reading more than one word at a time. Rather than letting your eyes rest on every single word, start looking at two words at a time, then three, and build up until you can read half a line at a time.

5. Read the summary, the conclusion, the introduction and scan major headings, graphs, charts and illustrations to save time.

6. Practise regularly.

Four Beliefs for Successful Speed Reading

■ Reading is easy.

■ It's OK to read using my finger.

■ I can read more than one word at a time.

■ I can read fast and comprehend what I'm reading.

Chapter 8

Nutrition and Learning

- The Importance of Protein

- Vitamins and Minerals

- Iron

- Fat

- Water

- Snacking vs Three Meals per Day

- What Can I Do in my Classroom?

Chapter 8

Increasingly, students are not eating the best foods to enhance learning. Proper nutrition can definitely boost thinking and learning.

The Importance of Protein

Protein is one of the most critical ingredients for the brain. Tyrosine, an amino acid found in proteins, enhances thinking and the brain uses this chemical to make electrically charged neurotransmitters such as dopamine and norepinephrine. These neurotransmitters are critical for alertness, quick thinking and fast reactions. They help with performing calculations, increase attention span and increase conscious awareness.

Unfortunately, many people typically have a breakfast which is high in carbohydrates such as toast, breads and cereals. Foods such as yoghurt, eggs, cottage cheese and fresh fruits are a better source of the nutrients necessary to enhance learning.

Some of the best high protein foods are soy beans, lean meat, nuts, cheese and eggs.

Vitamins and Minerals

Multivitamin supplements have a significant effect on learning according to researchers Benton and Roberts. Ninety twelve- and thirteen-year-olds taking a multivitamin supplement showed an increase in visual acuity, reactive time and intelligence over those who took a placebo. Obviously getting these nutrients from a natural source such as fresh fruit and vegetables is preferable. And, if possible, eat organic foods that are free of manufactured chemicals.

> Most people are digging their graves with their teeth.
>
> **Terry Roberts**

Studies in Germany, Finland and the University College in Wales showed that folic acid and selenium reduce depression and boost learner performance. Folic acid can be found in leafy green vegetables, but selenium is deficient in some soils. If necessary, it can be taken as a supplement in conjunction with vitamin E.

Iron

Iron is often discussed in learning circles as it increases mental activity (Jensen

1995). Iron-rich foods include pulses, meat, fish, eggs, dark green vegetables, grains and rice. To increase absorption of iron into the bloodstream these foods should be combined with vitamin C sources such as orange juice, broccoli and capsicum. Foods such as bran, cereals, soybeans, tea and coffee inhibit absorption. In fact, research has found that five times as much iron is absorbed into the bloodstream with a breakfast of orange juice, fruit and eggs as it is with cereal or bran, coffee or tea. Please note: food is always the best source of iron and children should never be supplemented with iron without pre-supplement blood testing.

> All bodily functions depend on water – the lack of it plays a major role in premature aging and disease.
>
> *What's the Big Deal about Water?*
> **Tonita d'Raye**

Fat

Drs Carol Greenwood and Gordon Winocur at the University of Toronto found that although the brain needs fats in order to be at its best, the type of fat is important. They found that a diet high in saturated fat slowed brain function. It is recommended that the diet includes polyunsaturated fats such as safflower, sunflower and soybean oils rather than saturated fats.

Water

Water is also essential for good health and success. Seventy per cent of the planet is covered with water, approximately 70 per cent of your body is made up of water and over 80 per cent of your brain is water. A lack of water can lead to dehydration which causes headaches, lack of concentration and focus, tiredness and many other challenges. It is recommended that adults drink at least eight glasses of water a day and children, four or five. It's just as important to keep up this intake in the winter as in the summer, as air conditioning and heat can dry us out even more than the sun. Again, provide opportunities for and encourage your students to drink water regularly throughout the day.

Snacking vs Three Meals per Day

What we eat affects our brains and our thinking. Alertness, memory, problem solving and emotional wellbeing are all affected by many different nutrients. How often we get these nutrients is also important. In a study published in the *New England Journal of Medicine*, students who ate seventeen snacks throughout the day had better cognitive functioning, fewer discipline problems and an enhanced sense of wellbeing over those who ate three meals throughout the day.

The Dunn and Dunn and MacMurren research models also reflect this. Teenagers were given the choice of either snacking during a test or not eating at all. Those who were permitted to eat the snacks (popcorn and raw vegetables) achieved significantly higher scores than the group who did not eat.

What Can I Do in my Classroom?

Many teachers are beginning to allow their students to eat during class. You may like to give students or parents a list of appropriate and acceptable food. Talk to your students about the positive role of nutrition and how it affects their performance, thinking and reaction times.

Too much time between eating can cause a loss of concentration and decreased alertness. This obviously has implications for skipping meals, especially breakfast.

Research suggests that blood sugar levels cycle every 45 minutes in young children and every 90 minutes in adults. This means that approximately 45–60 minutes after your students have eaten, their blood sugar level will be at a low and learning will be difficult. If you work with juniors you know they start asking, 'Is it playtime yet?' by about 9.45 a.m.

Some primary schools have changed their bell times to cater for this need. See timetable on page 87.

Morning tea and playtime has been renamed 'brain food break' to put the emphasis on the 'brain' food rather than the 'play' time.

Teachers using this timetable have reported focused students, an improvement in comprehension and a general sense of calm in their classrooms.

Some secondary schools have also changed bell times to avoid the after lunch syndrome of tired and/or hyperactive students due to their diet. Schools have two classes in the morning with a 20-minute break at approximately 11 a.m. Then two more classes until 1 p.m. Lunch is from 1 p.m.–2 p.m. and there is one class after lunch before home time. Teachers have reported students being more focused and attentive. Teachers have also said they enjoy the one hour after lunch.

A change in bell times ...

9 a.m.–10 a.m.

Class

10 a.m.–10.15 a.m.

Brain Food break

10.15 a.m.–11.15 a.m.

Class

11.15 a.m.–11.30 a.m.

Brain Food break

11.30 a.m.–12.30 p.m.

Class

12.30 p.m.–1.15 p.m.

Lunch (a slightly shorter lunch break cuts out the last 15 minutes when students are tired, bored and more likely to get into trouble)

1.15 p.m.–3.00 p.m.

Class (there is no break in the afternoon as most schools tend to include the less brain dominant topics such as P.E. and music in the afternoon)

Chapter 9

Emotions and Learning

- The Role of Emotions in Learning

- Value Every Effort

- Laughter Boosts Learning

The Role of Emotions in Learning

As educators we have often been focused on the physical environment within the classroom, but what about emotions in learning? Research now clearly shows that the emotional state your student is in is paramount for effective learning (Jensen 1994). A top researcher on emotions, N.H. Fridja, says that understanding learner emotions is one of the keys to motivation (Jensen 1998). Emotions influence:

- selective attention
- event interpretation
- motivation
- prediction

- recall
- decision making
- problem-solving
- learning

He states, 'when strong emotions are engaged, they so flavour the human experience that the learner is unable to bring anything else to conscious attention.'

As a teacher, attention needs to be given to the emotional state of your learners. Unless the learner is in a relaxed state of positive expectancy, very little of a constructive nature can happen. You have the power to influence the emotional state with activities that release stress or increase bonding or give the emotions a chance to be expressed.

> Behold the turtle – he only makes progress when he sticks his neck out.
>
> **James B. Conant**

The traditional education and teaching philosophy used to be: Keep things under control. Don't let students get out of hand. Suppress emotions. The new philosophy, based on the way the brain learns and takes in information, says: Engage emotions. Make learning compelling, fun and real.

How much do our emotions rule us? Just talk to anyone who is engaged in sales. Most salespeople will tell you the 'buying decision' is usually emotional. In fact, a top endorphin researcher at the US National Institute of Mental Health, Dr Candace Pert, says, 'The brain is just a little box with emotions packed into it.' (Jensen 1998)

Obviously there are different kinds of emotion. While your goal as an educator needs to be to create and engage positive emotions in the learning process, this may not always be reality in the classroom.

One of the key concepts I talk about at my 'Accelerating Learning and Boosting Personal Performance' workshop is that an alarming number of students are learning through the emotion of fear. Fear of failure, fear of being wrong, fear of appearing silly or even dumb in front of their peers.

Go into a new entrant classroom and watch the children. They are so keen to learn. They want to participate in everything. Watch as a teacher asks a question and hands go up to answer before the teacher has even finished asking. Participation is high. The students are keen, enthusiastic and want to learn. However, watch higher up in the school. The participation slows down and almost stops. Ask a group of year 6 students a question and several hands go up. Ask a year 11 class, and everyone looks at their desk. Fear sets in.

> The only failure is the failure to participate.
>
> ***Money & You* workshop**

When I facilitate workshops with adults and ask for a volunteer to come to the front of the room, I see the fear set in instantly. The internal voices are saying, 'I hope she doesn't choose me', 'What will I have to do?', 'What if I can't do it?', 'Will I look silly in front of my colleagues?'. It's the brave adult who raises their hand and offers to come forward.

An interesting acronym for FEAR is False Expectations Appearing Real. This is when learners recall a previous situation that didn't go the way they had anticipated (for example a failure) and imagine that happening in the future. They bring that experience to the present and make it real in their mind.

Tony Robbins uses a phrase that I think is essential thinking for learning and success, 'The past does not equal the future.' Just because you failed last year, yesterday or two minutes ago, doesn't mean you will fail on the next attempt.

What if Henry Ford, Einstein or Edison took this being scared of failure approach to their work. Edison, when inventing the light globe dealt with a body of distinguished experts who agreed that his efforts were 'unworthy of the attention of practical or scientific men'. (Don Fabun, *Three Roads to Awareness*) When a friend tried to console him after his 10,000 experiments with a storage battery failed to produce results, Edison replied, 'Why, I have not failed. I've just found 10,000 ways that won't work.'

Story after story can be found about successful people who have made mistakes and failed many times. One of my favourites is about Babe Ruth, an American baseball player. He holds the world record for number of home runs hit in his lifetime, 714. He also holds the world record for number of strike outs, 1330.

It is paramount to learning and success that you create an environment within the classroom that says, 'mistakes are OK'.

Value Every Effort

Valuing students' attempts and willingness to 'give it a go' is important. Celebrate the approximation at every level just as we do with babies. When they learn to walk, parents praise every tiny little improvement as well as each attempt.

Laughter Boosts Learning

Dr William Fry at Stanford University has discovered that the body reacts biochemically to laughing (Jensen 1994). Studies found an increase in white blood cell activity and changes in the chemical balance of the blood which may boost the body's production of the neurotransmitters needed for alertness and memory.

Students who laugh more learn more.

A good laugh can lower stress and a low-stress brain and body makes for a better learner. In the classic book, *Anatomy of an Illness*, Dr Norman Cousins revealed his laughter therapy which, he stated, was instrumental in his battle with cancer. The movie, *Patch Adams* (which is based on a true story), also illustrates this.

Chapter 10

Understanding the Brain

- Left and Right Brain

- The Triune Brain

- Mental Fitness

- Ages and Stages of Brain Development

- Reading and Writing: What's Appropriate

Chapter 10

Left and Right Brain

The two sides of the brain – the left and the right – have different functions. Obviously the brain is not that simplistic, but this is a useful model to use to begin to understand how you think, process and learn.

The left hemisphere is used for analytical operations, written and spoken langauge and logical processes. This side of the brain processes maths, reading, science and sequences, and is also where your short term memory is stored. The right hemisphere is involved with visualisation, synthesis and creativity. It is where you process colour, music, drama, feelings and long-term memory (Hannaford 1995).

> The greatest unexplored territory in the world is the space between our ears.
>
> **Bill O'Brien**

Left brain dominant people tend to be analytical, good at expressing themselves clearly, are well organised and see things in 'black and white'. These learners often prefer the step-by-step approach. Right brain dominant people tend to be intuitive, spontaneous, creative and adventurous. They can see shades of meaning, synthesise information effectively and remember easily. These learners often prefer a global approach to learning (Hannaford 1995).

Between the left and right sides of the brain is the corpus callosum, a thick bundle of nerve fibres that sends messages between the two hemispheres. When you access both sides of your brain in learning, learning is five times more effective (Hannaford 1995).

This can be achieved simply by using coloured pens when writing, or by listening to music (baroque) when doing maths. This is one of the basics of accelerating learning – using the whole brain to make learning more efficient.

The Triune Brain

Triune means 'three in one'. Our complex brain, as well as having a left and a right side, has three distinctive areas that also have different functions. The brain stem is an extension of the spinal cord. It controls your most basic instinctive responses. The brain stem monitors information from the senses in an automatic way and has a vital role in maintaining wakefulness. Its nerves are connected with all parts of the brain and the nervous system. The brain stem is joined to the cerebellum which coordinates information for smooth muscular movement. This part of the brain is commonly referred to as the reptilian brain.

The midbrain contains the thalamus, the hypothalamus and the limbic system. The limbic system controls your emotions and motivation, as it connects the 'instinctive' and 'rational' regions. Since emotional arousal is needed to activate attention and memory, the limbic system is probably a key to the learning sequence. The hypothalamus monitors the blood and controls your responses to hunger, thirst, oxygen needs and temperature changes. This keeps vital energy, water and oxygen flowing to the brain and the rest of the body.

The cortex, or neocortex, covers the midbrain, and is the most highly developed section. This is the thinking part of the brain, setting humans apart from the rest of the animal world. It controls use of language and symbols, analysis and synthesis, appreciation of art, music and any rational responses to external stimuli. It integrates information to build up overall pictures and to make connections with what is already stored. Most memory recall seems to come from large sections of the cortex.

When students experience any stress the brain automatically 'down shifts' from the neocortex to either the limbic or under extreme stress to the reptilian. As the neocortex deals with higher-order thinking, when a student 'down shifts', learning and memory are not so effective. Keeping the learning environment as stress free as possible will encourage more efficient learning.

Mental Fitness

Another way to develop the brain connections is through simple movements that switch on the brain. One such program is NLK Mental Fitness exercises from Neuro Linguistic Kinesiology.

These simple exercises help with the neurological organisation of the brain, helping to form efficient processing abilities. They help to reduce stress, enable students to become more centred, more coordinated and they make learning easier. Movements re-orient the electrical patterns of the brain and therefore defuse stress, clear the 'blocked circuits' and turn on the ability to learn.

Introduce this 5-minute switch-on into your daily routine. These exercises can improve spelling, writing, reading and listening. Children who find the X-crawl part of this activity challenging may also find reading and writing more difficult than their peers.

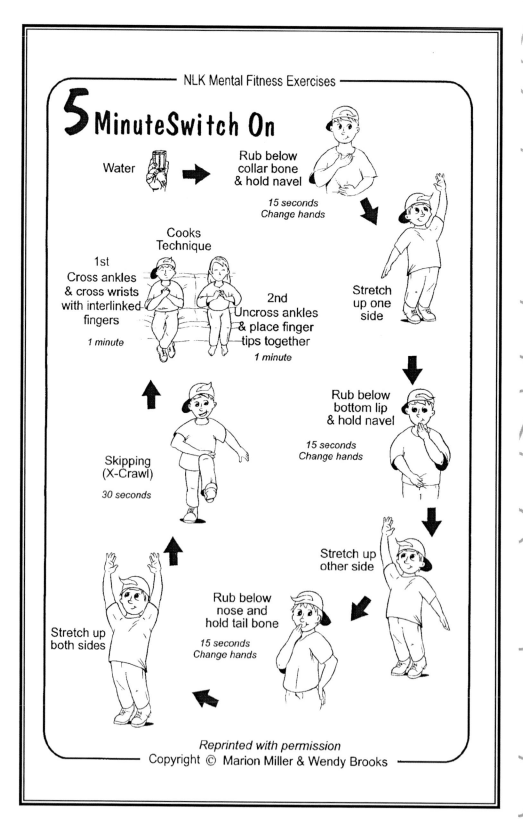

NLK Mental Fitness Exercises

5 Minute Switch On

Water → Rub below collar bone & hold navel

15 seconds
Change hands

Stretch up one side

Cooks Technique

1st
Cross ankles & cross wrists with interlinked fingers

1 minute

2nd
Uncross ankles & place finger tips together

1 minute

Rub below bottom lip & hold navel

15 seconds
Change hands

Skipping (X-Crawl)

30 seconds

Stretch up other side

Stretch up both sides

Rub below nose and hold tail bone

15 seconds
Change hands

Reprinted with permission
Copyright © Marion Miller & Wendy Brooks

X-Crawl:

1. Stand up and by raising your knees alternately, touch each hand to the opposite knee.

2. Do this about ten times.

3. Add some variations: with eyes closed, alternate elbows to opposite knee, alternate elbows to opposite ankle or heel, touch feet behind your back.

Children develop this skill of crossing the midline of the body usually between the ages of four and seven. This coincides with their learning to read and write. Encourage them to do the 5-minute switch-on routine as often as possible. They may choose any of the exercises to do any time they feel stuck.

Ages and Stages of Brain Development

Carla Hannaford's book, *Smart Moves* (1995), outlines the developmental ages and stages of the brain. These come from the work of Chris Brewer. By being aware of these stages and teaching to these, you will find a reduction in stress in your classroom and learning will become natural and easy.

An extract from *Smart Moves* by Carla Hannaford

Development of the cerebral cortex starts in the womb and continues until we die. Certain areas of the brain are feeding into the cerebrum at various times as natural development occurs. This is very much a continuous process but we can delineate a few landmarks. The following gives a 'ballpark' rather than exact developmental picture. We all naturally develop at our own pace in our perfect time.

Age (approximate): conception to 15 months

Development – Reptilian Brain. Basic survival needs – food, shelter, security and safety. Sensory development starting with vestibular system, then hearing, touch, smell, taste and finally sight – rich sensory activation. Motor development moving from reflexes to core muscle activation, neck muscles, arms and legs loading to rolling over, sitting, crawling and walking – motor exploration.

Age: 15 months to 4.5 years

Development – Limbic System/Relationship. Understanding of self/others, self/emotions, self/language. Emotional exploration, language exploration/communication, imagination, gross motor proficiency, memory development, social development.

Age: 4.5 years to 7 years

Development – Gestalt Hemisphere Elaboration. Whole picture processing/cognition, image/movement, rhythm/emotion/intuition. Outer speech/integrative thought.

Age: 7 years to 9 years

Development – Logic Hemisphere Elaboration. Detail and linear processing/cognition. Refinement of elements of language. Reading and writing skills development. Technique development in music, art, sports, dance, manual training. Linear math processing.

Age: 8 years

Development – Frontal Lobe Elaboration. Fine motor development – skills refinement. Inner speech – control of social behaviour. Fine motor eye teaming for tracking and foveal focus (2-dimensional focus).

Age: 9 years to 12 years

Development – Increased Corpus Callosum Elaboration and Myelination. Whole brain processing.

Age: 12 years to 16 years

Development – Hormonal Emphasis. Learning about body, self, others, community and meaningful living through social consciousness.

Age: 16 years to 21 years

Development – Refining Cognitive Skills. Whole mind/body processing, social interaction, future planning and play with new ideas and possibilities.

Age: 21+

Development – Elaboration and Refinement of the Frontal Lobes. Global/systems thinking. High level formal reasoning. Refinement of emotions – altruism, love, compassion. Insight. Refinement of fine motor skills.

We must get away from the notion that we simply experience the world until we go to school at the age of five and then we learn. Learning is a progressive, constantly changing process that serves to enrich and expand our understanding through our life. The neocortex is always growing neural networks linked to the brain stem and limbic system, developing the neural connection that enables it to become the integrator of knowledge.

> Children learn when the brain is ready.

Even at the age of about 21, there is a growth spurt of nerve net development in the frontal lobes. It's the time when people realise their parents are smarter than they thought, as emotional refinement allows for insight leading to altruism and love.

There is also another spurt of growth at approximately thirty with further refinement of muscle movement, especially of the hands and face. Increased fine motor coordination leads to greater achievements for musicians like pianists and violinists who can move their fingers with more agility. We also see it in vocalists who are now able to command a greater range with their vocal cords (muscles). And we see it dramatically in character actors who can now control their facial muscles with such subtlety that they express any emotion with just their faces (Hannaford 1995).

Reading and Writing: What's Appropriate

In the usual course of development, children are accessing right brain function at the time they traditionally begin attending school, at about age five. The right hemisphere of the brain begins development and enlargement between the ages of four and seven, while the logic hemisphere doesn't enlarge until ages seven to nine. The most natural way, then, for children to learn when first at school at age five and six is through image, emotion and spontaneous movement.

What age group are you teaching and how can you teach to the natural development of the brain? When processes are taught before the brain is ready, it often causes stress, making learning harder.

Chapter 11

Developing Intelligence

- Lateral Thinking

- What is Intelligent Behaviour?

- Multiple Intelligences

Chapter 11

Lateral Thinking

Thinking outside the box and looking for solutions from different angles is a skill that is responsible for our ingenuity. It is also a skill that, as you face more complex challenges in your life, will allow you the flexibility to think through and provide solutions for particular situations.

Many of the major shifts in our society have come from such lateral thinking. For example, in the early nineteenth century it was believed that the only way humans would travel faster was to breed faster horses. However, though attempts were made to build better carriages or breed faster horses, no major breakthroughs were achieved. It wasn't until the invention of the steam train that people could travel faster and more efficiently.

In 1930, Michael Cullin revolutionised shopping with the concept of customers helping themselves to the goods on the shelves in the first chain of supermarkets. Lateral thinking can be used to solve challenges in education, business, social and family life. So how do you look at challenges from a different angle? How can you teach your students to think laterally, outside the box?

There are four steps to lateral thinking, according to Paul Sloane:

1. **Test assumptions**. There is a saying that 'assume' makes an ASS out of U and ME. Jumping to conclusions without weighing up all the facts restricts our ability to solve challenges. Assumptions can be useful. If you see smoke coming under a door it is sensible to assume there is a fire on the other side and to test the door before opening it and ring the fire brigade. In Brazil a car thief used people's assumptions to his advantage. When cars stopped at the traffic lights he would throw a snake in the open driver's window. The driver would jump out of the car, assuming the snake was poisonous, and the thief would jump into the car and drive away. The snake turned out to be harmless.

   When solving challenges test your assumptions by asking simple questions. Restate the puzzle in a slightly different way. Dropping false assumptions is not as easy as it sounds.

How many squares can you see?

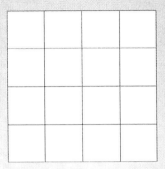

There are 16 small squares, one big one, 4 small squares make a medium square (and there are 9 of these) and 9 small squares make a medium large square of which there are 4, so there are 30 squares in total.

Sometimes what we see first may not be the true potential. This is often the case with students. What we often see and deal with in the classroom is the behaviour but what is the true potential of the student?

Have a go at this puzzle. If you have seen this before resist the urge to say, 'I know this one.' Just do it again – you may be surprised at your result.

Using 4 straight lines, connect all 9 dots. Each line must pass through each dot once. Once you start, your pencil must stay on the page. (See solution on page 107)

2. **Ask broad questions**. Start with broad questions to narrow down the possibilities. As you get closer to the solution ask more detail-oriented questions. For example, if I asked you to guess the number I'm thinking of between 1 and 100, a wide question would be, 'Is it more than 50?', 'Is it an odd number?', 'Is it divisible by 3?' Detailed questions are more of the rifle shot approach, 'Is it 32?' This strategy will take longer and is not as efficient.

   When solving challenges establish a broad framework of what happened or could happen and then move into more specific details.

3. **Be creative**. Until 1968 Olympic high jumpers rolled over the bar face down. In 1968 an American, Dick Fosbury, introduced a new approach, the 'flop', leaping over with his back close to the bar and face up. Up until then he was ranked 48th in the world. Using this new technique he won the gold medal. Today, nearly all top jumpers use this method.

4. Logical Thinking. To be great at lateral thinking you also need to be good at thinking logically. This means using the information you already have to correctly figure out the answer by asking intelligent questions and checking assumptions. Combining the open-minded, imaginative approach to problem-solving with the skills of logical analysis and reasoning forms the basis of really successful lateral thinking.

What Is Intelligent Behaviour?

Technology is growing rapidly and the accelerative change that is happening in our world is phenomenal. According to Tom Polland from Entrepreneurial Success Programs (2000), information doubles every 18 months and maybe even faster. The students you work with are entering a unique time in history. No longer can you give them the skills for specific jobs or employment. A statistic published in the *Dominion* newspaper during September 1999 stated that New Zealand had 295 centenarians at the time. It was estimated that by the year 2050 there will be 9000 people over the age of 100! Who knows what the world will look like then.

What you can give your students is the learning strategies that promote intelligent behaviours and lead to lifelong success.

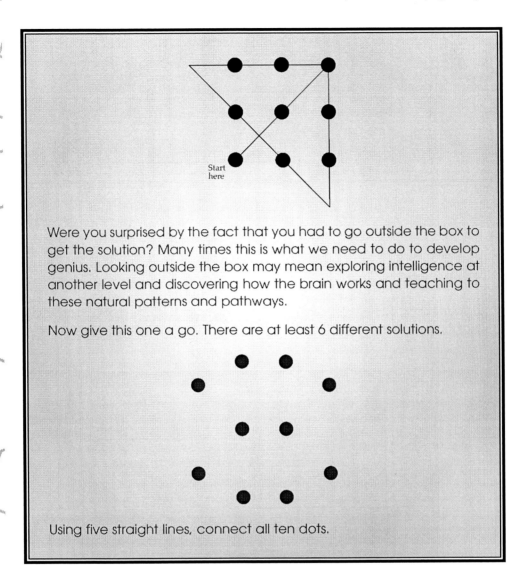

Were you surprised by the fact that you had to go outside the box to get the solution? Many times this is what we need to do to develop genius. Looking outside the box may mean exploring intelligence at another level and discovering how the brain works and teaching to these natural patterns and pathways.

Now give this one a go. There are at least 6 different solutions.

Using five straight lines, connect all ten dots.

One of the world's leading experts in intelligent behaviour is Art Costa. Following are twelve characteristics that he promotes as intelligent behaviours that can be taught and observed (Costa & Kallick 2000).

1. Persistence

This is what happens when the going gets tough. Students often say, 'I can't do this,' or 'It's too hard,' so they don't have to think any further. Encourage perseverance by teaching at least three ways to solve a problem so students have a backup if one strategy doesn't work. The more ways you have to solve a challenge, the more likely you are to keep going.

Teaching Ideas

An ideal activity to cultivate specific language is to practise giving directions and instructions.

■■■

Nurture risk-taking in your students. Accept all ideas and reward creativity.

ооо

Encourage students to identify the feelings of others and how it might feel to be in someone else's shoes.

●●●

Invite students to set and pursue goals.

✦✦✦

Encourage students to describe how they feel about a certain issue or topic.

◆◆◆

Teach students there is more than one way to solve a problem.

♪♪♪

Encourage students to consider all possibilities and consequences of actions before beginning a task.

■■■

Encourage students to think about how they arrived at their answers and conclusions.

❖❖❖

Provide opportunities for students to proofread their own work.

☺☺☺

Link new learning to real-life situations.

2. Managing Impulsiveness

Impulsive students often blurt out answers and make immediate value judgements. Encourage students to consider possibilities and consequences of actions before they begin a task. After giving an instruction, Art Costa suggests asking, 'What would you be doing if you were following the instructions correctly?' I have frequently had success managing impulsiveness with the phrase, 'In a moment, but not quite yet …'

3. Listening to Others with Understanding and Empathy

Some psychologists believe that the ability to listen to another person, to empathise with and understand their point of view is one of the highest forms of intelligent behaviour. We spend 55 per cent of our life listening, yet listening is rarely taught. Teach students how to paraphrase and ask clarifying questions. Encourage students to set aside their own views as they listen to others. Ask questions such as 'If you were … how would you think about …?'

4. Flexible Thinking

Some students have difficulty considering alternative points of view. Their way is the only way. Teach students that not everything is black and white – there is also a rainbow in between. Use words and phrases such as 'however,' 'on the other hand' or 'if you look at it this way'.

5. Metacognition: Awareness of our Own Thinking

What is thinking? What does it mean to think hard? There is no common definition of thinking. Ryan, a ten year old, suggests, 'Thinking is what nature hired the mind to do.' Another child suggested it was, 'What you do when you don't know the answer.' Up to 50 per cent of people are not aware of their own thinking processes while they are thinking. When asked, 'How did you solve that problem?' they may answer, 'I don't know; I just did it.' Invite students to tell you *how* they arrived at the answer rather than focusing just on the answer.

How can you develop intelligent behaviour in your classroom?

☐ have faith that all your students can think

☐ set goals of education in terms of intelligent behaviours

☐ challenge students to perform higher-order thinking with questions and imagination

☐ create a safe, risk-taking environment

☐ give it time – change is not a quick fix – plan to develop intelligent behaviours over a three to five year period

☐ provide a rich, responsive environment

☐ meet students' needs according to their developmental readiness and sequence

☐ model the behaviour you want from your students – set an example they can follow. As Emerson said, 'What you do speaks so loudly I can't hear what you're saying.'

6. Checking for Accuracy and Precision

As technology grows at a rapid rate, the need for accuracy and precision grows. Ninety-nine per cent accuracy for air traffic controllers is not acceptable. In the past, students handed in work and teachers checked for accuracy. Encourage students to recheck their own work – over and over. It often helps to leave it a day and then go back over it. Invite students to check each other's work as well. It's often easier to locate other's errors than your own. When marking work, instead of giving a mark of say 7/10, write, 'There are three errors on this page. Please find them.'

7. Questioning and Problem Posing

Sometimes students are reluctant to ask questions for fear of appearing ignorant. The more a student questions, the more curious they become, leading to enhanced imagination and improved memory and intelligence, according to Robert Sternberg (1990). Encourage students to ask, 'What good questions did I ask today?' rather than 'What did I do today?'.

8. Drawing on Past Knowledge and Applying it to New Situations

Art Costa (2000) advocates that probably the ultimate goal of teaching is for the students to apply school-learned knowledge to real life situations. Intelligent human beings learn from experience. They are able to make meaning from one experience and apply it in a new situation. Phrases such as 'this reminds me of …' and 'this is like the time I …' are common with students who display this intelligent behaviour.

9. Precision of Language and Thought

Be alert to sloppy language such as non-specific words like 'nice', 'OK', 'good' or names of objects like 'stuff', 'junk' and 'things'. You might hear 'They told me' or 'everyone has one'. Promote specific language. Ask students to come up with many other words they can use to name or describe.

10. Using All Senses

Foster the use of all five senses – sight, sound, touch, smell and taste – where appropriate. Provide activities that involve several senses. The more sensory pathways that are open in our students the more information they can absorb.

Teaching Ideas

Provide thoughtful debates between students.

❀❀❀

Create crosswords with key ideas from your lessons.

❖❖❖

Encourage students to discuss concepts with others.

∮∮∮

Allow students to keep a journal of their learnings and to write stories.

⊙⊙⊙

Use storytelling to explain concepts.

♦♦♦

Invite students to write a newsletter, booklet or dictionary about new learnings.

✦✦✦

Tell stories from your own experiences and allow students to tell their stories.

◆◆◆

Read, tell or create poetry.

ooo

Tell jokes.

❖❖❖

Write creatively and read to students often.

11. Ingenuity, Originality and Insightfulness

Increasingly it is becoming apparent that the capacity to generate novel, original or clever ideas, products or solutions are skills that can be developed. Intelligent humans are creative. They solve problems and challenges using lateral thinking. Creative people take risks and test their own limits. They are often intrinsically rather extrinsically motivated.

12. Wonderment, Inquisitiveness, Curiosity, Enjoyment of Problem-Solving

A student who has an 'I can' attitude is heading towards success. More than this, creating a learning atmosphere where students enjoy learning is paramount to intelligent behaviour. Encourage the sense of wonderment at the small things such as a dew drop on a leaf and the inquisitiveness and curiosity of 'why'. Make the learning process more enjoyable and important than the outcome or answers. It's the journey that counts, not the destination. Wonderment, awesomeness and passion are prerequisites for intelligent behaviour, says Art Costa.

Multiple Intelligences

Howard Gardner, a professor of neurology at Boston University Medical School, maintains that there are eight basic kinds of intelligence and that most people – especially when encouraged – develop strengths in at least one (Gardner 1993). Schooling and IQ tests focus on two of these intelligences – the linguistic and the mathematical. But, says Gardner, the other six – the musical–rhythmic, visual–spatial, bodily–kinesthetic, naturalist, interpersonal and intrapersonal – deserve attention, too. Hardly any of us shine in all eight intelligences, so it is important to appreciate those we have rather than lament over those we don't.

Gardner suggests making a conscious effort to include all eight intelligences into your teaching, at least once a day in primary classrooms and once a week for secondary students. It can be as simple as asking the students to make up a four-line song to review a topic, or providing reflective time for journal writing, providing group discussion or adding a problem-solving dimension to your subject.

Teaching Ideas

Encourage computer programming as this is a very logical process.

♦♦♦

Draw flow charts and pie graphs.

Provide number sequences to solve and pattern games.

☺☺☺

Encourage problem-solving and inventing new ideas and concepts.

❖❖❖

Allow students to predict and analyse information.

●●●

Use Venn diagrams to explain concepts.

■■■

Invite students to make a timeline of their life.

○○○

Use guided imagery and visualisations.

Encourage painting and drawing to express ideas.

ᴓᴓᴓ

Teach mind mapping as a skill for note taking and idea generation.

♦♦♦

Allow pretending and play.

✦✦✦

Use sculpting to express information and ideas.

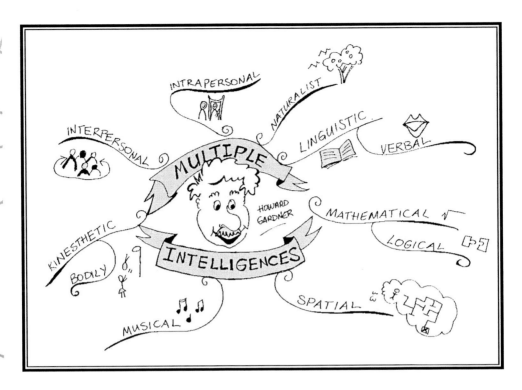

Verbal–Linguistic Intelligence

Verbal–linguistic intelligence involves the spoken and written word and sign language for a variety of purposes such as entertaining, persuading, communicating ideas, solving problems, reading instructions and writing poetry, novels, articles and so on.

People who have strong verbal–linguistic intelligence like to read and write, enjoy talking and have an extensive vocabulary (these people are usually good at crosswords). As the name suggests, verbal–linguistic people can often speak, or pick up quickly, a new language and they enjoy word games and rhymes.

Do you: ask lots of 'why' questions?

Do you: enjoy talking?

Can you: speak more than one language?

Can you: complete crossword puzzles?

Games and activities that enhance this intelligence include *Scrabble*, *Boggle*, *Password*, *Trivial Pursuit*, *Up Words* and *Wheel of Fortune*.

Teaching Ideas

Provide or make jigsaw puzzles with key lesson concepts.

✦ ✦ ✦

Create and read cartoons.

♦ ♦ ♦

Create films and videos of work. This is great for revision later.

ℒℒℒ

Invent a board or card game to demonstrate knowledge and understanding.

❋ ❋ ❋

Provide opportunities for singing, dancing and rapping. This is an excellent way to revise information.

○ ○ ○

Encourage students to perform ideas to others.

■ ■ ■

Collect and present songs about your topic.

● ● ●

Present a short class musical to another class.

❖ ❖ ❖

Encourage students to listen to environmental sounds.

☺☺☺

Write music and create songs.

☉ ☉ ☉

Write and perform jingles.

Logical–Mathematical Intelligence

This intelligence involves recognising and exploring patterns, categories and relationships using symbols or objects. It is also experimenting and problem-solving, prediction and analysis and is a step-by-step logical process.

Can you: easily work out how many weeks it is to your birthday?

Do you: enjoy solving puzzles?

Do you: want to know how things work?

Are you: interested in 'if … then' logic?

Games and activities that enhance this intelligence include *Monopoly*, backgammon, cribbage, dominoes, *Mastermind*, 21, *Othello*, *Triomino*, *Leverage* and *Cashflow*.

Visual–Spatial Intelligence

Visual–spatial intelligence is the ability to perceive and manipulate three dimensional objects or visual materials in your head. It also involves knowing where your body is in space and the relationship between items.

Can you: walk from one end of your house to the other in the dark – without having to run your hand down the wall?

Can you: put the leftover dinner in exactly the right sized container?

Can you: parallel park a car easily?

Are you: good at drawing, painting or constructing?

Do you: have a keen eye for detail?

Games and activities that enhance this intelligence include *Battleship*, draughts, chess, chinese checkers, *Connect Four*, *Pictionary*, *Memory* and noughts-and-crosses.

Teaching Ideas

Provide physical exercise at least once a day.

♦♦♦

Use drama, mime and role-playing to emphasise learning.

Teach folk and creative dance.

☺☺☺

Encourage students to play sports and games.

❖❖❖

Use task and puzzle cards for reinforcing concepts.

●●●

Invent a board or floor game to reinforce learning.

■■■

Keep plants and animals in the classroom that the students take responsibility for.

○○○

Conduct hands-on experiments.

Use the outdoors as a classroom.

ℒℒℒ

Encourage students to collect and mount natural specimens.

◆◆◆

Allow students to use magnifiers, microscopes and binoculars.

Musical–Rhythmic Intelligence

Musical–rhythmic intelligence is the ability to communicate or gain meaning from music. In combination with bodily–kinesthetic intelligence, it is being able to respond to and create music. Musical–rhythmic intelligence also involves sensitivity to patterns in sound. Plato believed that musical understanding was an essential element of thinking and consequently recommended that children should be taught music before any other subject. Through attending to the rhythm and harmony of the music, he contended, children would develop minds that would be able to process other types of information.

Can you: sing in tune?

Can you: move rhythmically?

Are you: sensitive to sound patterns?

Do you: enjoy musical experiences?

Do you: play or create music?

Games and activities that enhance this intelligence include *Encore: The Memory Game of Lyrics and Laughs, Musical Trivial Pursuit, Simon* and *NoteAbility: The Name-the-Song Game*

Bodily–Kinesthetic Intelligence

This intelligence involves the use of motor skills for tasks such as playing sport or dancing. It is also provides the fine motor skills used for calligraphy and cross-stitch or manipulating tools.

Do you: have a good sense of balance?

Do you: have excellent hand-eye co-ordination?

Are you: good at sports?

Do you: enjoy physical exercise?

Games and activities that enhance this intelligence include *Jenga*, pick up sticks, tiddlywinks, *Twister* and charades.

Naturalist Intelligence

Genius is 1 per cent inspiration and 99 per cent perspiration.

Thomas Edison

People who have the ability to recognise and classify the flora and fauna species of an environment are said to have this intelligence.

Do you: spend lots of time outdoors?

Do you: collect plants, rocks or animals?

Are you: interested in outdoor sounds?

Do you: notice relationships in nature?

Games and activities that enhance this intelligence include scavenger hunts, orienteering.

Teaching Ideas

Take students to the zoo.

✦✦✦

Encourage peer teaching of new concepts.

ооо

Provide group work and opportunities for students to interact with others.

◆◆◆

Practise giving and receiving feedback. Teach listening skills and understanding someone else's point of view.

◉◉◉

Encourage sharing of feelings and ideas.

ℒℒℒ

Conduct class meetings.

■■■

Provide time for silent reflection, journal writing and self-assessment.

❖❖❖

Use guided imagery and self expression through art.

Interpersonal Intelligence

Interpersonal intelligence involves sensitivity to feelings, motives and moods of others. It involves an ability to build relationships with others and to work as a team. It is also being empathetic towards others.

Can you: walk into a room full of strangers and have a conversation with someone?

Are you: a team player?

Do you: relate well to peers?

Do you: display leadership qualities?

Are you: empathetic to others?

Games and activities that enhance this intelligence include *Dungeons and Dragons*, *Family Tree* and group simulations.

Intrapersonal Intelligence

This is being aware of your own feelings, ideas and thoughts. It is recognising your own pattern of strengths and weaknesses and knowing how to maximise your strengths.

Can you: go to a movie by yourself?

Can you: communicate your feelings?

Are you: confident in your own abilities?

Do you: set appropriate goals?

Games and activities that enhance this intelligence: Solitaire, Patience, solo simulation games

'Kids make their mark in life by what they can do, not what they can't,' says Howard Gardner. 'School is important, but life is more important. Being happy is using your skills productively, no matter what they are' (in Lasear 1991).

Chapter 12

Teacher Success Tips

- Time Management

- Dealing with Stress Effectively

- Sleep

Chapter 12

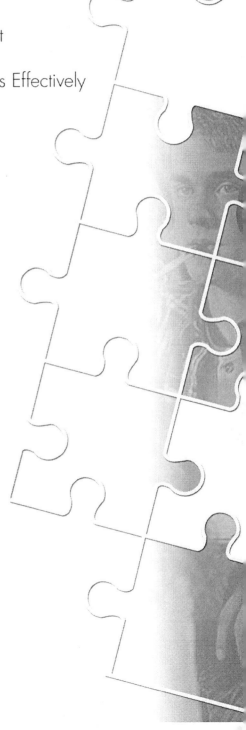

Time Management

There is sometimes a fine line between failing and succeeding. People who fail often work as hard as those who succeed. One of the major differences, according to Robyn Pearce, author of *Getting a Grip on Time,* is that successful people are more focused and effectively prioritise.

Know What's Important

Decide what is most important and concentrate on these tasks until completed. Avoid getting stuck in the urgency trap. Plan regularly to avoid rushing and adding extra pressure.

Set Goals

Set yourself clear goals and refer to them regularly to make sure you're on track.

Weekly Planning

Spend at least fifteen minutes a week planning the week ahead. What are your personal and work goals for this week?

Daily Planning

Prioritise what is important on a daily basis. Choose a maximum of five tasks to complete each day and score them in order of importance. Start with number one and work through the list. If you complete these before your day is over, you can take a break or you may wish to prioritise another three tasks for the rest of the day. If you don't complete these, transfer them to the list for the next day.

Avoid Time Wasters

People often major in minor things. Here's a couple of ideas to avoid time wasting. Handle each piece of paper once and then file it. Selectively read information and throw out anything that is not useful.

Bank of Time

Imagine there is a bank that credits your account each morning
with €86,400. It carries over no balance from day to day.

Every evening it deletes whatever balance you failed
to use during the day.

What would you do?

Draw out every cent, of course!

Each of us has such a bank.

Its name is TIME.

Every morning, it credits you with 86,400 seconds and every
night it writes off, as lost, whatever of this you have failed
to invest to good purpose.

It carries over no balance.

It allows no overdraft.

Each day it opens a new account for you.

Each night it burns the remains of the day.

If you fail to use the day's deposits, the loss is yours.

There is no going back.

There is no drawing against the 'tomorrow'.

You must live in the present on today's deposits.

*Invest it so as to get from it the utmost in health,
happiness and success!*

The clock is running. Make the most of today.

On the telephone, keep conversations to the point and use an answering machine when you're busy. A helpful way to end a conversation is to stand up – even when you're on the phone.

Delegate Tasks

This is the art of gaining time by effectively involving others. I often think, 'What is the best use of my time right now?' Then I delegate the tasks that are not as important. Keys to effective delegation include describing the task and the required result in detail and giving a completion time. If necessary demonstrate the task and then leave the person alone to complete it.

One Thing at a Time

One of the most powerful time management tools I have learned is that I can only do one thing at a time. Concentrate on this before moving on to the next task. Become result oriented, not action oriented.

To realise the value of a YEAR, ask a student who failed an exam.

To realise the value of a MONTH, ask the mother of a premature baby.

To realise the value of a WEEK, ask the editor of a weekly newspaper.

To realise the value of an HOUR, ask the people waiting to meet.

To realise the value of a MINUTE, ask a person who missed the train.

To realise the value of a SECOND, ask a person who just avoided an accident.

To realise the value of a MILLISECOND, ask the person who won silver in the Olympics.

Dealing with Stress Effectively

Stress is normal. It is a healthy response of the body and it is useful to remind us to stop and rest. It can also be a motivating factor behind getting projects finished as the deadline gets closer. What is not normal is regular, prolonged and excessive stress. It decreases your immune system, making you more likely to get sick and burnt out. Here are some effective ways of dealing with stress:

1. Create time each day just for you

It may only be five minutes but make it a priority. Things to do include walking around the garden; sitting and reading a book; stopping near a pond, river or the sea on your way home; having a bubble bath; spending time with loved ones including your pets; sitting in the sun.

2. Seek out mentors

Surround yourself with positive people who energise you. Discuss how they manage daily stress.

3. Get quality sleep

It doesn't have to be eight hours – quality is better than quantity. Learn how to maximise your sleep as this is the time you are recharged and re-energised.

4. Eating well

A leading expert on nutrition, Dr Kathrine Davis, recommends 9+ servings of fruit and vegetables per day to maximise health and minimise stress on the body. Avoid eating heavily two hours prior to bedtime as digestion takes energy that could be used for recharging and rejuvenating (Davis 2001).

Treasure every moment

And remember that time waits for no one.

Yesterday is history

Tomorrow is mystery

Today is a gift

That's why it's called the present!

---

5. Reduce negative influences

Avoid the daily news on TV, radio and in the paper as it is normally filled with negative stories. Unfortunately, positive news doesn't sell well. Avoid people who are negative and often full of gloom and doom. They just bring you down.

6. Delegate tasks

This one can be challenging, however even if the person only does your tasks 70 per cent as well as you would, your stress levels will halve.

7. Remove pages from your diary

This is one of my favourites and perhaps one of the hardest to do. Removing a day or two a month ensures you cannot book any meetings. Have the day off and indulge yourself. As a teacher, book afternoon appointments with yourself. This means you can't book anything else during this time.

8. Exercise regularly

People who exercise at least three times a week enjoy less stress because gentle exercise increases the chemical serotonin, which calms you and strengthens your immune system.

9. Leave work at work

This is easier said than done. The opening of *The Simpsons* TV show has Homer bringing home radioactive material. Do you? Stay on an extra 30 minutes or an hour when it's quiet and then when you get home, you can decompress by taking a shower or changing your clothes.

10. Smile

Ever tried to feel sad or stressed while you're smiling?

Sleep

An important part of coping with stress is ensuring adequate and good quality sleep. This is the time your body recharges and rejuvenates ready for the next day. Following are seven suggestions for a better night's sleep.

1. Relax before bedtime

Put the challenges of the day to one side to calm your mind. If this is difficult, writing them down is a good idea. Read to relax, however it's best to choose a good, but reasonably dull, book. Horrors and thrilling mysteries can re-stimulate the brain. Other ideas include listening to music, having a warm bath or doing some gentle yoga or stretches.

2. Establish a pre-sleep routine

This will signal to your mind and body that now is the time to sleep. You probably have a series of tasks you complete each night such as brushing your teeth, setting the alarm clock, turning off the lights, locking the house, closing windows etc. To help you sleep, these activities should be performed in the same order every night.

The 'Big Rocks' of Life

One day as an expert on the subject of time management stood in front of a group of high-powered over achievers he said, 'Okay, time for a quiz.' Then he pulled out a 5-litre, wide-mouthed jar and set it on a table in front of him. Then he produced about a dozen fist-sized rocks and carefully placed them, one at a time, into the jar. When the jar was filled to the top and no more rocks would fit inside, he asked, 'Is this jar full?'

Everyone in the class said, 'Yes.'

Then he said, 'Really?' He reached under the table and pulled out a bucket of gravel. Then he dumped some gravel in and shook the jar causing pieces of gravel to work themselves down into the spaces between the big rocks.

Then he smiled and asked the group once more, 'Is the jar full?'

'Probably not,' one of them answered. 'Good!' he replied. And he reached under the table and brought out a bucket of sand. He started dumping the sand in and it went into all the spaces left between the rocks and the gravel. Once more he asked the question, 'Is this jar full?'

'No!' the class shouted. Once again he said, 'Good!' And he grabbed a pitcher of water and began to pour it in until the jar was filled to the brim. Then he looked up at the class and asked, 'What is the point of this illustration?'

One eager beaver raised his hand and said, 'The point is, no matter how full your schedule is, if you try really hard, you can always fit some more things into it!'

'No,' the speaker replied, 'that's not the point. The truth this illustration teaches us is: If you don't put the big rocks in first, you'll never get them in at all.'

The title of this story is The 'Big Rocks' of Life. What are the big rocks in your life? A project that YOU want to accomplish? Time with your loved ones? Your faith? Your education? Your finances? A cause? Teaching or mentoring others? Remember to put these BIG ROCKS in first or you'll never get them in at all.

So when you are reflecting on this story, ask yourself this question: What are the 'big rocks' in my life? Then, take action and put those 'big rocks' in your jar first ... now!

Author Unknown

3. Exercise early

Daily exercise helps release tension and energy and improves sleep. Research, however, shows that vigorous exercise just before bed does not improve your sleep. You may feel tired but your body is actually revved up. Your heart, brain and other organs, stimulated by exercise, need time to cool down. If you want to exercise to increase your sleep, exercise earlier in the day. The ideal form of exercise is aerobic and includes walking, jogging, dancing, swimming and skipping. The key is to choose an activity you enjoy and make it a habit. Regular exercise can help you feel better, look better and sleep better.

> If you don't look after yourself, who will?

4. Avoid caffeine

Caffeine stimulates the body and brain and can disturb sleep. Research suggests that on average, people who have two cups of coffee a day spend a longer time trying to get to sleep (Kavey 1996). Caffeine's effect can last up to six hours so avoiding it in the evening is important. Remember caffeine is also found in tea, chocolate, cola drinks and most of the 'smart' energy drinks.

5. Snack lightly before bedtime

Yes, you do feel sleepy after a big meal, but eating heavily does not aid the sleep process. Have a light snack 30 minutes before going to bed. Food suggestions include fresh fruit, cottage cheese, cashew nuts, toast, a bowl of cereal and herbal teas such as chamomile.

6. Find the right temperature

Room temperature can make a huge difference to your sleep quality. Not too hot and not too cold is important. Dress for the temperature you prefer and use layers of sheets and blankets to control the temperature.

7. Take a morning walk

Exposure to light, particularly in the early morning can actually help you sleep at night. Light resets your biological clock. Timing of this light is crucial. Your body clock is most responsive to sunlight in the early morning between 6 a.m. and 8.30 a.m. Direct sunlight for 30 minutes is the best according to research. Lack of sunlight can trigger seasonal affective disorder (SAD), a form of depression. The effects of sunlight are greatest when combined with physical activity.

Amabile, Teresa, 1989, *Growing Up Creative*, Crown Publishers Inc., New York, USA.

Benton, D. & Roberts, G., 1998, 'Effects of Vitamin and Mineral Supplementation on Intelligence of a Sample of Schoolchildren, *Lancet*, no. i, pp. 140–143.

Costa, Art & Kallick, Bena, 2000, *Habits of Mind: A Developmental Series*, ASCD, Virginia, USA.

Cousins, Norman, 1991, *Anatomy of an Illness*, Bantam Books, USA.

Davis, Kathrine, 2001, 'Corporate Nutrition', Women in Business Conference, Auckland, New Zealand.

De Porter, Bobbi & Hernacki, Mike, 1997, *Quantum Business: Achieving Success through Quantum Learning*, Dell Publishing, New York, USA.

Dunn, K & Dunn, R, 1978, *Teaching Students through their Individual Learning Styles: A Practical Approach*, Reston Publishing, Virginia, USA.

Fabun, Don, 1971, *Three Roads to Awareness*, Glencoe Press, California, USA.

Gardner, Howard, 1993, *Frames of Mind*, Fontana Press, London, UK.

Greenwood, Carol & Winocur, Gordon, 'Cognitive Impairment in Rats Fed High-Fat Diet: A Specific Effect of Saturated-Fatty-Acid Intake', *Behavioural Neuroscience*, June, vol. 110, no. 3, pp. 451–9.

Grinder, Michael, 1991, *Righting the Education Conveyor Belt*, Metamorphous Press, Oregon, USA.

Hannaford, Carla, 1995, *Smart Moves*, Great Ocean Publishing, USA.

Hill, Napoleon, 1996, *Think and Grow Rich*, Random House, New York, USA.

Jensen, Eric, 1994, *The Learning Brain*, Turning Point Publishing, USA.

Jensen, Eric, 1995 *Super Teaching*, Turning Point Publishing, USA, pp. 28–32.

Jensen, Eric, 1998, *Teaching with the Brain in Mind*, ASCD Publications, USA.

Jukes, Ian, 2003, 'Digital Kids: Learning in a Digital Landscape', www.infosavvey.com.

Kavey, Neil, 1996, *50 Ways to Sleep Better*, New American Library, USA.

Kehoe, John, 1994, *Mind Power*, Zoetic Inc., Canada.

Kiyosaki, Robert, 1992, *If you Want to Be Rich and Happy ... Don't Go to School*, Aslan Publishing, USA.

Knight, Sue, 1995, *NLP at Work*, Nicholas Brealey Publishing, London, UK.

Laborde, GenieZ, 1994, *Influencing with Integrity*, Syntony Publishing, USA.

Lazear, David, 1991, *Eight Ways of Knowing*, Hawker Brownlow Education, Melbourne, Australia.

North, Vanda & Buzan, Tony, 1991, *Get Ahead: Mindmap your Way to Success*, Buzan Centre Ltd, Dorset, UK.

Pearce, Robyn, 1996, *Getting a Grip on Time*, Reed Books, New Zealand.

Polland, Tom, 2000, Entrepreneurial Success Workshop, Auckland, New Zealand.

Robbins, Anthony, 1991, *Awaken the Giant within*, Simon and Schuster, New York, USA.

Rose, Colin, 1987, *Acceleratd Learning*, Dell Publishing, New York, USA.

Rosenthal, Robert, 1992, *Pygmalion in the Classroom*, Crown House, USA.

Sousa, David, 2002, *How the Brain Works*, Corwin Press, California, USA.

Sternberg, Robert, 1990, *Beyond IQ: A Triarchical Theory of Human Intelligence*, Yale University Press, New Haven, USA.

Sugars, Brad, 1998, Entrepreneur Workshop, 26–29 November, Brisbane, Australia.

Underwood, Margaret, 1995, Learning Styles workshop, July, Wellington, New Zealand.

Ward, Christine & Daly, Jan, 1993, *Learning to Learn*, self-published, Christchurch, New Zealand, pp. 27–29.

Wohlfarth, Harry, 1984, 'The Effects of Color-Psychodynamic Environmental Modification on Disciplinary Incidences in Elementary Schools over One School Year: A Controlled Study', *The International Journal of Biosocial Research*, vol. 6, no. 1, pp. 44–53.

Books

Armstrong, Thomas. *Seven Kinds of Smart*. Penguin Group, USA, 1993.

Armstrong, Thomas. *Awakening Genius in the Classroom*. Association for Supervision and Curriculum Development, Virginia, 1998.

Buzan, Tony. *The Mind Map Book*. BBC Books, London, 1993.

Chilton Pearce, Joseph. *Magical Child*. Penguin Group, New York, 1992.

Coory, David. *Stay Healthy by Supplying What's Lacking in Your Diet*. Zealand Publishing House, New Zealand, 1995.

Edwards, Betty. *Drawing on the Right Side of Your Brain*. HarperCollins, London, 1993.

Hannaford, Carla. *Smart Moves*. Great Ocean Publishers, Virginia, 1995.

Jensen, Eric. *The Learning Brain*. Turning Point Publishing, USA, 1995.

Jensen, Eric. *Brain-Based Learning*. Turning Point Publishing, USA, 1996.

Jensen, Eric. *Teaching with the Brain in Mind*. Association for Supervision and Curriculum Development, Virginia, 1998.

Kiyosaki, Robert. *If You Want to Be Rich and Happy, Don't Go to School*. The Excellerated Learning Publishing Co, USA, 1992.

Knight, Sue. *N.L.P at Work*. Nicholas Brealey Publishing, London, 1995.

Kroehnert, Gary. *Taming Time*. McGrawHill, Australia, 2000.

Margulies, M.A. *Mapping Inner Space*. Zephyr Press, Tucson, 1991.

Miller, Marion & Brooks, Wendy. *NLK Mental Fitness Exercises*. Marion Miller, New Zealand, 1999.

Parker, Allan & Stuart, Margaret. *Switch on Your Brain*. Hale & Iremonger Pty Ltd, Sydney, 1986.

Parore, Lee. *Corporate Edge*. Celebrity Books, New Zealand, 1998.

Pearce, Robyn. *Getting a Grip on Time*. Reed Publishing, New Zealand, 1996.

Robbins, Anthony. *Unlimited Power*. Simon & Schuster Ltd, London, 1986.

Robbins, Anthony. *Awaken the Giant Within*. Fireside, New York, 1991.

Rose, Colin. *Accelerated Learning*. Dell Publishing, New York, 1987.

Sloane, Paul. *Test Your Lateral Thinking IQ*. Sterling Publishing Company Inc., New York, 1994.

Schwartz, David. *The Magic of Thinking Big*. Simon & Schuster Inc., New York, 1987.

Vialle, Wilma & Perry, Judy. *Nurturing Multiple Intelligences in the Australian Classroom*. Hawker Brownlow Education, Australia, 1995.

Walker, Morton. *The Power of Colour*. Avery Publishing Group Inc., New York, 1991.

Ward, Christine & Daly, Jan. *Learning to Learn*. Christine Ward & Jan Daly, New Zealand, 1998.

Tapes

The Gift of Self Esteem (series of six tapes)

Entheos … The Sustaining Power of Enthusiasm by Glen Capelli

Personal Power 30 days – The Driving Force by Anthony Robbins

Notes